PENGUIN BOOKS

IT WAS A DARK AND STORMY NIGHT

Scott Rice is a professor of English at San Jose State University and the creator of the Bulwer-Lytton Contest. Born in Lewiston, Idaho, and raised in Spokane, Washington, he received his B.A. from Gonzaga University and his M.A. and Ph.D. from the University of Arizona. Scott Rice is married and the father of three children: Jeremy, Matthew, and Elizabeth.

EDWARD BULWER-LYTTON

IT WAS A DARK AND STORMY NIGHT

The Best (?) from the Bulwer-Lytton Contest

Compiled by
SCOTT RICE

Penguin Books

PENGUIN BOOKS

Viking Penguin Inc., 40 West 23rd Street, New York, New York 10010, U.S.A.
Penguin Books Ltd, Harmondsworth, Middlesex, England
Penguin Books Australia Ltd, Ringwood, Victoria, Australia
Penguin Books Canada Limited, 2801 John Street,
Markham, Ontario, Canada L3R 1B4
Penguin Books (N.Z.) Ltd, 182–190 Wairau Road,
Auckland 10, New Zealand

First published in Penguin Books 1984
Reprinted 1984, 1985 (three times), 1986, 1987
Published simultaneously in Canada

LIBRARY OF CONGRESS CATALOGING IN PUBLICATION DATA
Main entry under title:
It was a dark and stormy night.
1. Authorship—Anecdotes, facetiae, satire, etc.
2. Fiction—Technique—Anecdotes, facetiae, satire, etc.
3. English language—Sentences—Anecdotes, facetiae, satire, etc.
4. English language—Style—Anecdotes, facetiae, satire, etc.
5. Style, Literary—Anecdotes, facetiae, satire, etc.
I. Rice, Scott.
II. Title: Bulwer-Lytton Contest
PN6231.A7718   1984   818'.5408   84-11141
ISBN 0 14 00. 7556 9

Printed in the United States of America by
R. R. Donnelley & Sons Company, Harrisonburg, Virginia
Set in Caslon
Designed by Beth Tondreau

CONTENTS

INTRODUCTION

From January to April of 1983 the English Department at San Jose State University sponsored the Bulwer-Lytton Fiction Contest, an unorthodox literary competition that asked its entrants to compose the opening sentence to the worst of all possible novels. Ultimately, the contest attracted more than 10,000 entries from all over the United States and from nearly fifty foreign countries. The winning entries included in this book (except for the 1984 winner on p. xiii) are from the 1983 contest. In addition to inspiring this "literary" outpouring, the contest also prompted numerous questions about its own nature and origins. The following were among the most commonly asked.

Q. Just what exactly was the Bulwer-Lytton Contest?

A. The Bulwer-Lytton Fiction Contest was a bad-writing contest, one that pitted the entrants against the worst literary minds in bookdom. The goal of each entrant was to compose the worst possible opening sentence for an imaginary novel. In other words, the contest asked for the worst words, for intentionally bad prose.

Q. What is the purpose of having such a contest?

A. The contest was created to fill a need. Most literary contests are inherently unfair, favoring as they do talent, sensibility, and intelligence. They are snooty affairs that only encourage the tyranny of the talented, rewarding a favored few by perpetuating a *talentist* chauvinism. They are callously neglectful of the mediocre masses, those who might be authors if they had any craft, vision, or message.

Q. But isn't it the proper task of English teachers to encourage people to read and write good books?

A. That is all very well and good, but what about all those who would rather write bad books than read good ones? And besides, there are already more good books than a normal person can expect to read in a lifetime. Whenever someone writes another good book, it just creates a lot of anxiety for those who are afraid they will never find the time to read it.

Q. Why ask for only one sentence?

A. We figured that most people have short-winded muses.

Q. Whom was the contest named after?

A. The contest was named after Edward George Earle Bulwer-Lytton (1803–1873), a prolific Victorian novelist and a general all-around man of letters. As a writer of novels he was second in popularity only to Charles Dickens. In fact, a keen judge of public taste (or tastelessness), he reputedly convinced Dickens to alter the ending of *Great Expectations,* arranging for its hero, Pip, to get married and live happily ever after. In Victorian England this was known as good box office.

Q. What did Bulwer-Lytton do to merit the honor of a contest in his name?

A. He has been an inspiration to generations of untalented writers, the most famous of whom is Snoopy in the *Peanuts* comic strip. It was Bulwer-Lytton in his novel *Paul Clifford* (1830) who introduced the notorious opening line "It was a dark and stormy night." This is, of course, the line with which Snoopy always opens his novels. (A much better writer, Madeleine L'Engle, also used it to open *A Wrinkle in Time.*) Having created a standard for bad openings with his line, Bulwer-Lytton alone deserves to have such a contest named after him.

Q. What is so bad about "It was a dark and stormy night"?

A. Aside from being a little obvious and melodramatic, not too much, if Bulwer-Lytton had stopped there. Unfortunately, he went on:

It was a dark and stormy night; the rain fell in torrents—
except at occasional intervals, when it was checked by a
violent gust of wind which swept up the streets (for it is in
London that our scene lies), rattling along the housetops,
and fiercely agitating the scanty flame of the lamps that
struggled against the darkness.

Even by Victorian standards the sentence will not win any
prizes for economy or subtlety.

Q. Is the rest of the novel written in the same manner?

A. Sometimes it is even worse. In the very next sentence a character is "wending his solitary way." Later in the novel a fellow lighting his pipe is described as "applying the
Promethean spark to his tube," a glass of beer is "a nectarian
beverage," and a bedroom is "a somnambular accommoda-
tion."

Q. Did Bulwer-Lytton write any novels that we in the late twen-
tieth century might remember?

A. That depends on whether you remember *The Last Days of
Pompeii*, his most widely read and reprinted novel. It has been
made into three movie versions, once with Preston Foster,
once with the cinema strong man Steve Reeves, and most recently for TV.

Q. Were the movies as good as the book?

A. A cinematic rarity: all three were.

Q. Did Bulwer-Lytton do anything else that should make us
mindful of him?

A. He coined the expression "the great unwashed," and if you
consult your *Bartlett's Familiar Quotations,* you will see that he
is also responsible for the phrase "The pen is mightier than
the sword" (from a play called *Richelieu,* about the famous
French prelate).

Q. Was Bulwer-Lytton's pen mightier than the sword?

A. On a good day, maybe mightier than a letter opener.

Q. Is *anybody's* pen mightier than the sword?

A. Putting aside consideration of whether the pen could ever be mightier than an Uzi submachine gun, read the entire quotation:

> Beneath the rule of men entirely great,
> The pen is mightier than the sword.

Q. What inspired Bulwer-Lytton to write novels in the first place?

A. His mother. Disapproving of his choice of a wife, she cut off his allowance. Most authors write out of sheer love of the language and from the desire to uplift and enlighten their fellow creatures; Bulwer-Lytton did it to pay the rent.

Q. Honestly now, was Bulwer-Lytton really so bad that he should have a wretched-writing contest named after him?

A. Although he perpetrated that famous opening, he wasn't all that awful. He did write some gripping tales, in spite of the fact that his characters were wooden, his plots relied heavily on improbable coincidences, and his diction was gratuitously polysyllabic. Some literary critics like to credit him with introducing the historical novel as we know it, a carefully researched work that attempts a circumstantially authentic picture of an earlier time. He traveled to Italy to gather material for *Rienzi* and *The Last Days of Pompeii*. His last two novels about English history—*Harold, the Last of the Saxon Kings* and *The Last of the Barons*—are also well researched by the standards of the day. Some students of the occult also regard three of his works as classics: *A Strange Story, Zanoni,* and *The Coming Race.*

Q. How do you get a hyphenated name?

A. If you are Edward George Earle Lytton Bulwer, you assume your mother's family name when you inherit her estate.

Q. What would Bulwer-Lytton himself have thought about having a bad-writing contest named after him?

A. Any ambitious would-be artist worth half his salt would prefer notoriety to neglect. Since the contest began, Bulwer has gained dozens of new readers.

Q. Why have a contest that rewards bad writing? Isn't there enough putrid prose in the world?

A. The contest did not actually encourage *bad* bad writing, but *good* bad writing, writing so deliberately rotten that it both entertains and instructs. Bad is only bad when it thinks it is good or, worse, doesn't care. Actually, the contest was like other literary competitions in one key respect: it rewarded writers who achieved their desired effects. In this case, the effects were intentionally bad, but they required control over materials. Compare the entrants to someone impersonating a drunk on ice skates.

Q. Who judged the contest?

A. A panel of undistinguished judges consisting of those most willing and qualified—unpublished authors, self-appointed arbiters, and envious backbiters.

Q. Who entered such a contest?

A. The perverse, the profane, and the whimsical. More precisely, convicts and clergymen, schoolchildren and school superintendents, electricians and librarians, photographers and physicians, servicemen and CPAs, painting contractors and investment counselors, housewives, househusbands, and house painters. Most contestants fell into two classes, though: good writers pretending to be bad writers, and bad writers pretending to be good writers pretending to be bad writers.

Q. Why would anyone want to enter a bad-writing contest?

A. To enjoy the forbidden delights of untrammeled wordplay, to make ironic Orwellian statements about the value of proper language, to forge in the smithies of their souls the uncreated conscience of their race—in short, to get attention.

Q. A small question—who won?

A. Gail Cain of San Francisco won in 1983; Steve Garman won in 1984. The winning entries appear on the following page.

Q. What were the worst words worth?

A. The original plan was to offer fellowships not to write, but there was one niggling objection—no money. Ultimately, the 1983 winner was awarded the Snoopy Prize, a "dark and stormy night" cartoon panel autographed by Charles Schulz; the 1984 winner received a word processor. On the runner-up we inflicted the complete works of Bulwer-Lytton, a gift calculated to make the nights long if not dark and stormy.

The camel died quite suddenly on the second day, and Selena fretted sulkily and, buffing her already impeccable nails—not for the first time since the journey began—pondered snidely if this would dissolve into a vignette of minor inconveniences like all the other holidays spent with Basil.

—*Gail Cain*
San Francisco, California
1983 *Winner*

The lovely woman-child Kaa was mercilessly chained to the cruel post of the warrior-chief Beast, with his barbarian tribe now stacking wood at her nubile feet, when the strong clear voice of the poetic and heroic Handsomas roared, "Flick your Bic, crisp that chick, and you'll feel my steel through your last meal."

—*Steve Garman,*
Pensacola, Florida
1984 *Winner*

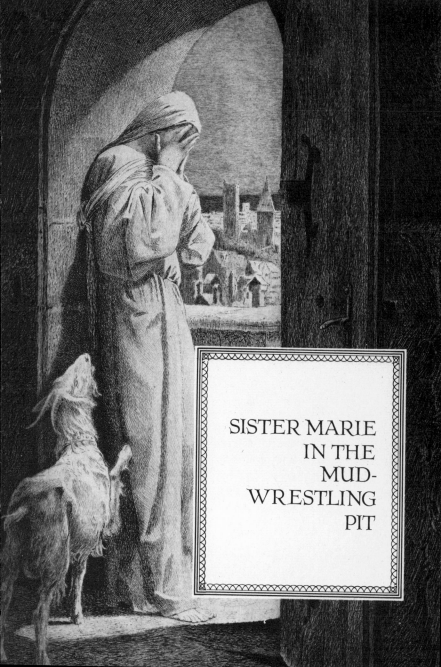

SISTER MARIE
IN THE
MUD-
WRESTLING
PIT

AND IF THAT DOESN'T APPRISE YOU, NOTHING WILL!

"The celebrated name which forms the title to this work will sufficiently apprise the reader that it is in the earlier half of the fourteenth century that my story opens." —opening sentence of
Rienzi; or, The Last of the Tribunes (1835)

As she fell face down into the black muck of the mud-wrestling pit, her sweaty, three-hundred-pound opponent muttering soft curses in Latin on top of her, Sister Marie thought, "There is no doubt about it: the Pope has betrayed me!"

—Richard J. Savastio
Media, Pennsylvania

The very last thing that Mary Immaculata, the newly appointed mother superior at Saint Gertrude's Convent, would have expected as she approached Pius IX Hall was that the cherub-cheeked novice Maureen Shannon who stood atop the steps to greet her was, in reality, and had been for three years, Rocco Genardi, a boy. *—John Paul Vancini*
Brooklyn Center, Minnesota

Serenity lay over the grounds like a soft caress; the bells for matins chimed as they had for centuries before as seventy-five black-robed nuns rose from their cots and licked their lips in an-

ticipation of Sister Immaculata's cinnamon Wheatena, which
steamed comfortingly in the refectory.   —*Mary A. Harrison*
Marietta, Georgia

Sister Mary Agnes coughed, spit a gobbet of blood, and tossed
the severed goat's udder over the rim of the canyon.
—*Charles F. Mason, Ph.D.*
North Bend, Oregon

Father Braun opened the cover of the new missal, scraped his
cuticle on the razor edge of the frontispiece, and slumped in the
corner of the confessional.   —*Ted Erskine*
Cleveland, Ohio

The familiar dimness of the confessional offered no comfort to
Father Flanagan; unused to truly shocking confessions, the
young priest had difficulty in providing appropriate spiritual guid-
ance to the despicable criminal who had just admitted his role in
engineering the astounding heist of the Vatican treasure—and
the father's problems were magnified by the realization that this
confessor (if he but knew it) was the one person in the world who
could resurrect the past which haunted the slender young cleric:
Derrick O'Malley, who could reveal Father Flanagan's dark secret—that the priest was in reality a transsexual named Monica
O'Malley—Derrick's sister!   —*Nancy Linder*
Madison, Wisconsin

"Prune in June, Mr. Goodwrench," urged the inflamed rabbi,
wiping the cornstarch off his brow and squinting knowingly at
the sun, a mere ninety-three million miles away; "we're talking
geraniums here, not generators, and no matter how damp things
get, no matter how preposterously burdensome these damp

things become, no matter how repugnantly foul these things appear, it will take more than a fistful of Krugerrands to persuade me to entrust my prized potpourri of perennials to you and your genuine GM parts!"   —*Eunice Pro*
Sierra de Fuego, California

Castrated, frustrated, and inundated with blessings, the young high priest of the lowlands bowed his head to the winds of love and looked down the long, lonely street of life to an unconsummated dream just beyond the pale, having turned the emollient, proverbial corner with his vows of celibacy, nevermore to embrace his beloved Herr Dresser.   —*Diane Redus Holcomb*
Sperry, Oklahoma

Although our efforts were valiant and full of a grace surpassing all flaw, our time served as missionaries of the Middlepuddle Indians had finally run out as we found ourselves fleeing from the onslaughts of the illiterate bastards—God be our witness!
—*Stephen R. Villanueva*
San Jose, California

The besotted Rev. McNeely was his own congregation in the toy cathedral called Army of the Cross Tabernacle, and in the dank, lugubrious undertones of guilt emanating from its cryptlike candlelit interior he found himself its sole living denizen, entombed there with the effigy of his Savior, who was enshrined over the altar, pinned to a stick of pine like a voodoo doll that has served its purpose.   —*E. T. White*
(Jonathan E. Boys)
Sargentville, Massachusetts

LIKE AN
OVERRIPE
PEACH IN A
BLENDER

ACTUALLY, IT WAS THE MORNING OF A HARD, COLD DAY IN DECEMBER, BUT WHAT THE HELL!

"It was the evening of a soft, warm day in the May of 17—."   —opening sentence of
The Disowned (1828)

Dawn Esterbrooke looked lovingly upon the gifts which her lifelong childhood friends brought to her wedding shower, but inside her guts churned like an overripe peach in a blender because only two hours earlier she had left a motel with her best friend's homosexual father.   —*Steve Garman*
Pensacola, Florida

Tenderly their eyes looked over the dinner table which, laden with wine as cold as his wife's heart and bread as hot as his new mistress's passion, threatened to split asunder, leaving their viands embarrassingly on their laps.
—*Caryl Stock*
Chapel Hill, North Carolina

When Michael S. Lapka, the greatest unpublished writer in the world, had finished the last draft of his first novel, it was like polished marble; you could see the veins, blue and purple, under the surface, and you could tell that they were real, they were his.
—*Don Austin*
Vancouver, British Columbia, Canada

The floating boy, who felt as placid as a green lagoon, bobbed like a buoy in the bay, which was as calm as a sleeping child, while toddlers on the beach cried and built castles in the sand, eating gritty, mustardy hot dogs, while the sun burned in the sky like an orange-tinted iodinized blister and, as gauze around the blister, gossamer clouds made ephemeral patterns, much in the same way, but not quite exactly like the very way, that water vapors would.
—*Mary K. Bradford*
Daly City, California

It was autumn, and the fog clung to the old house as it did nearly every autumn (with the exception of the previous year, which had been incredibly sunny) like damp gauze on a soldier's wound, except that there was no blood, as he stopped the car at the curb and gazed thoughtfully towards the house.
—*Rebecca V. Swaidan*
Ventura, California

A sky the color of old bruises hung over the dry, ever-reaching stretches of the Australian outback.
—*Christine Veith*
Girard, Pennsylvania

Like the Parthenon at dusk, Grandma Riggleman stood in the middle of the cornfield watching a squadron of honking Canadian geese tugging the warm blanket of night over the last August harvest of her life.
—*Andrew C. Towers*
Clayton, Michigan

Like the tail of a receding comet, the intensity of its light waning in incremental decrements with the distance, or like the whistle of a freight train, moaning a Dopplerian threnody, so the

memory of his boyhood dreams flitted briefly through his consciousness as he fell asleep.   —*David L. Stephens*
Winston-Salem, North Carolina

With an abandoned gesture that brought a flush to the face of the passing blonde, virile, six-foot-two J.B. hurled his vicuña, silk-lined coat onto the backseat and, grinding out his cigarette with the toe of his calfskin boot, he sank—as if sinking into the arms of his mistress—into the spotted leopard nylon fur of the low driving seat of his Italian sports car, while almost instantaneously letting in the clutch and slamming his foot greedily, orgasmically onto the accelerator, so that the luscious car gasped in surrender and enjoyment, gathered itself together like a great cat, and obediently shot forward round the first corner like an arrow plunging into the heart of Saint Sebastian.

—*E. L. Summers*
London, England

The battered coupe accelerated like a pregnant water buffalo, rode like a three-legged gazelle tumbling down an escalator, and handled like a Doberman on acid; but it had gotten Bobby-Bob out of a jam here and a tight spot there, and he'd be damned if those city slickers would turn it into Zippo lighters.

—*Don Stacom*
Rowayton, Connecticut

He watched as his fishing line disappeared into the murky, brown water in which green algae was so thick it formed green swirls, giving the appearance of lime sherbet curling its way through a scoop of chocolate ice cream.

—*Robert R. Johnson, Jr.*
West Salem, Wisconsin

Jhijhi's long blonde California hair cascaded over her face like a frozen waterfall of Chablis blanc, but when Lance—unless it was Gregory, or Pablo, or hopefully not her landlord—venomously hissed, "Who?" she exposed one sea-blue eye and the tip of her coral tongue and peripherally pouted, "What?"

—Lysander Kemp
Harwich Port, Massachusetts

The rain splattered down on the tables of the café like raisins dropped by uncaring gods. *—Patricia A. Folkerth*
Columbia, South Carolina

Marvin gazed fondly after Meribel, her marvelously mobile parts filling her clothes the way milk fills a bucket, and sloshing seductively down the rosy hall, which glowed like a maid on a sailor's lap. *—Sharon V. Brown*
Los Gatos, California

Her face was lined like a patchwork of meandering rivers strung together over a bed of waffles. *—Don Stacom*
Rowayton, Connecticut

Dawn broke like a crusty suet pudding, leaving greasy colorless clouds stuck like cotton balls on the gunmetal gray sky.

—Joan B. Cotta
San Jose, California

Nurse Daniels smelled like good Italian bread.

—Sharron Cohen
Gloucester, Massachusetts

Wallowing on the divan like a prize pig in the mud, Dixie re-evaluated her seemingly sordid life at the Laundromat.
—*James Sheldon Averbeck*
Cincinnati, Ohio

With as little energy and as much false hope as a lobster kept alive in a restaurant window, Peter Richards awoke and did his few small meaningless exercises.
—*Don Austin*
Vancouver, British Columbia, Canada

From the moment she entered, Moira O'Hanlon's tawdry elegance galvanized the Back Bay ballroom, the luminescence of her Galway-green eyes and the heat rising from her voluptuous cleavage drawing the tuxedoed Brahmins like derelicts to a Bronx trash-can fire on a cold Saint Valentine's Eve.
—*Anthony Buckland*
Vancouver, British Columbia, Canada

Lucinda, virginal still but her soul violated by Jeffrey's lust, lay on the moon-raped sand iridescent in her pain, scattered in a limbo screaming in the silence, her love hanging around her shredded soul like a piece of tattered silk, clinging to her body like tarnished velvet, all hope dropping from her destroyed life like unraveled knitting, when suddenly the thought came to her that tomorrow is another day, and the broken virgins of her dreams that moments before had been like scattered petals beyond repair were salvaged by her haunted mind and the phantom of her fantasy was, after all, still alive as she brushed the moon-touched tears from her pale cheeks and started back to the château.
—*Cornelia P. Hunt*
San Francisco, California

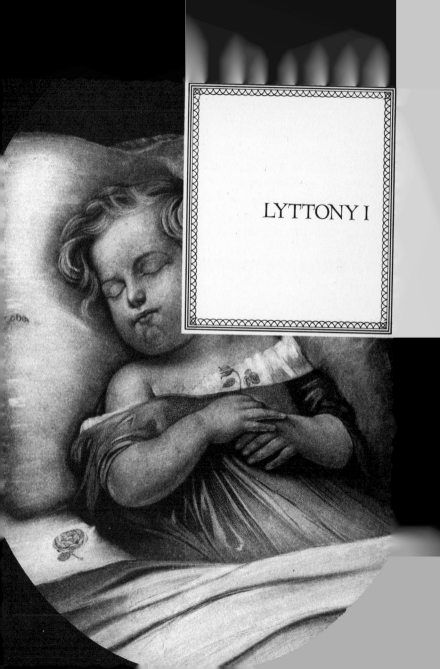

LYTTONY I

WE'D BETTER HOPE HE INHERITS HIS MOTHER'S BRAINS AND HIS FATHER'S LOOKS!

" 'Sir—sir, it is a boy!'
" 'A boy,' said my father, looking up from his book, and evidently much puzzled; 'what is a boy?' "

—opening sentences of
The Caxtons (1849)

"It could well be that you will not leave here alive," I suggested, as I slipped back the action on my Vikki Weber 38–06, spilling all six bullets onto the floor. —*Ralph Holmstad*
Sausalito, California

It was a singular day at Chez Maurice, a chichi restaurant in a not so chichi part of the city, when Miranda clutched madly at her throat, gurgled those impossible words, and expired, while John, not yet in the position of sleuthing, but an intuitive sort, unbuttoned her blouse and found the letters—well, it's not at a point in the story where they can be revealed—engraved in permanent ink upon her chest. —*Susan Harrow*
San Francisco, California

Millard Fillymissolimp (who was otherwise known as Joe) stepped into the room where his great-grandfather Colonel Douglas Moran of the Fourteenth Idaho Light Cavalry Dragoons was assassinated on April 2, 1852, by an enraged sergeant

major of drummers who was aiming for someone else entirely but was apparently a very lousy shot, and asked for a glass of wine, which was bottled in the wonderful Bordeaux region of France, where the sky is deep blue and the hills are vibrant green and the sea isn't there and the people are often drunk, but was quickly refused.
—*Mark Key*
Englewood, Ohio

The man stood in an abyss of cerebration ruminating pensively on the ebon thunderhead impending extermination of the dark-blue suede empyrean with all its glittering, silver jewels and decided that it was going to rain.
—*Mary A. Byrne Solari*
Burbank, California

"The variety of quirks, ailments, and miscellaneous disfigurements that can strike the average supermarket shopping cart is truly amazing," she said.
—*Gertrude Ruth Radfar*
Fort Lauderdale, Florida

Only one front wheel of the shopping cart turned; the other was frozen by dried egg yolk.
—*Peggy Bishop*
Burbank, California

For eight or nine hours on a dull, dark, and variably cloudy day around the third week of September, with the forecast saying there was an 85 percent chance of precipitation, I was driving a

beat-up '68 Chevy through New Jersey when all of a sudden
around six or six-fifteen it hit me that I was within view of the
melancholy House of Usher, but I missed the exit and decided to
keep on driving to Trenton.   —*Manson Campbell*
                                        Sewickley, Pennsylvania

On his face was a map of the ould sod, in his eye a leprechaun's
twinkle, in his tongue a gift of the blarney and a taste for a wee
nip of the poteen, and, while not one to pick a fight, he thought
there was nothing like a good donnybrook to bring men together.
                                        —*David L. Stephens*
                                        Winston-Salem, North Carolina

Step. Drag. Step. Step. Step. Drag. Despite the shooting pain,
he held his head high, pride glowering in his large, brown eyes;
he was, after all, a Lippizaner.   —*Joanne Siegmann*
                                        New York, New York

The Highly Detailed Historical Research Novel

Naruma's drindle sac revealed the bulge of a velvet
placottine beneath the leather strappings of his broadcloth
gurneyboard which, though made of woolsey and vat-
dyed to the deep shade of the arliss flower, characterized
his class far more than the brieviartkin which graced his
brow.   —*Nancy J. Miller*
                                        Needham, Massachusetts

"My God!!! It's ALIVE!!!!" cried the nubile young lab assistant, whose sensitive baby-blues cast a knowing glance away from the microscope to the grotesque hunchback drooling darkly in the corner, so overwhelmed with searing passion she didn't hear the shot ring out or the maid scream, or notice the delicate scent of magnolia blossoms drifting in through the portholes of the saucer hovering over the plantation, thinking only of the previous night, when Harry Hungstud had thrown her naked on the bed and forced—yes, FORCED!!!—her to caress his motorcycle boots with her tongue, for in her consuming ambition to be chairman of the board of Intergalactic Perfumes, Inc., there was no depravity, no perversity, no unspeakable descent into utter animal self-degradation that Harriet would not endure.

—*John J. Pollock*
San Jose, California

H. CALIBER, INVESTIGATIONS

HAVING EARLIER DIVESTED TOLEDO...

"It was the summer of the year 1491, and the armies of Ferdinand and Isabel invested the city of Granada."
—opening sentence of
Leila; or, the Siege of Granada (1838)

Musing on his impossibly short cigar, the fat, balding painter was admiring the just-completed lettering on my opaque glass door, "H. Caliber, Investigations," when she glided into the office, aloof, elegant, reeking of money and gratified whims, one of those precise women whose lipstick and nail polish match, in hue and intensity, one of the tertiary colors in her muted and multicolored silk scarf (which came first, I wondered, the lipstick or the scarf?).
—Jerry Heifferon
San Jose, California

The silent aperture, round, breathless, speechless, frozen above a stiff jaw, spoke him dead.
—Georges Allaire
La Pocatière, Quebec, Canada

After thirteen years on the force your gut tells you more than your brain, and when his bloodshot, hound-dog eyes saw the skinned corpse of the world's most famous dolphin, once the most popular animal on television and now left for the swimming vultures of the gulf to devour, he knew something both sinister and perverted was at play.
—Steve Garman
Pensacola, Florida

There was only one thing anyone was certain of: three young women were lying dead in the morgue, all murdered in the same way, and no one seemed to know what to do about it; no one, that is, except Bubba Brown, the gap-toothed, red-headed, freckle-faced eight-year-old son of the local barber—but no one listened to gap-toothed, red-headed, freckle-faced eight-year-old boys, so he just went about in his quiet, eight-year-old way, gathering clues and solving the case himself and very nearly getting killed in the bargain. —*J. Thompson*
Rochester, New Hampshire

Famed amateur sleuth Lord Douglass Whimpp, monocle in place, dressed appropriately in tweeds with scarlet cravat, which had been selected by his trusted servant Codge (a man of impeccable taste), hastened to his chauffeur-driven Rolls, which was parked in front of Leverby Hall, and drove rapidly to the exclusive Marzipan Club (an organization composed of elderly career military types) only to find the body of Colonel (retired) Sir Frederick Fortesque-Jones, DSC, OBE, lying covered with blood on the library floor with a half-empty glass of gin and bitters by his side and a revolver clutched in his left hand, attended by Subaltern Percy Smythe, who was engaged to his daughter Lady Belinda with every anticipation of June nuptials to be performed by the Archbishop of Pottsbury-on-the-Rye, Reginald Blatt, who had devoted his religious career to the conversion of the aristocracy. —*Joan Northcott*
Palo Alto, California

Detective Sergeant Thudley Snigger pedaled manfully down the narrow, unmetaled—and therefore decidedly mucky—lane that led to the very minor village of Skinny Dipping, Dulcet,

pondering the possible kinetic effects of removing his training
wheels.   —*Ann M. Williams*
                                        Westlake Village, California

I pounded down the crap-slick alleyway, clutching the Luger
as it belched out its last hunk of white-hot metal, which tore at
the elusive sonuvabitch sidestepping at full speed ahead of me,
while screeching, marauding cats scattered and clattering gar-
bage cans spilled their guts, missed the bastard, and slammed into
the brick wall. (from *I, The Fury*)   —*G. B. Johnson*
                                        Walnut Creek, California

"One more step, Butcherman, and I'll blow your friggin' head
across the street," I muttered hoarsely, feeling the weary, who-
gives-a-shit letdown that hits me like a ton of bricks whenever I
wrap up a case.   —*Sharron Cohen*
                                        Gloucester, Massachusetts

He had had that dream before and it now froze him to his bed,
breathing heavily, his soiled Nikes gleaming gaudily from one
corner of the elongated, blue-toned, carpeted room; there would
be no slumber this eve, sleep's stark shadows would have to wait
the dawn; yet he couldn't call Sarah—no, not at this hour, nor
Rosebud, Pete, or Sammy-O, or even Maxie, poor, dear "Fat
Maxie," no, he'd call them all in the morning.

                                        —*Bill Deiz*
                                        Portland, Oregon

It was a sticky yellow dawn as I awoke and slowly lifted my
pounding head, with thoughts of thanks to the Big Guy in the sky
instead of a gripe over my continual slug-out with a sinus prob-

lem, from a crusted puddle of barf left over from a late-night celebration with a pretty good bottle of bourbon and a dumb dishwater-blonde lady companion of the C-note variety, a celebration of yet another case successfully cracked by yours truly, Ace Callahan, Private Eye.
—*Dave Visbeck*
Brentwood, California

There are things a good detective can feel in his bones, and Dillon Shane knew Jesimine Kimberly Collinsworth did not drown in her sleep on New Year's Eve.
—*Frances H. Shaw*
Saint Petersburg, Florida

Mitch Moribundus wasn't a pleasant guy—his face could scare a troll—so when his daughter, Helen the Hooligan, got snatched in broad daylight outside Greasy Fred's Sushi Bar and Bawdyhouse, the smart money said "mob hit" and everyone in the tiny Queens seashore community went about their business as usual—except the one man who suspected the truth, Murray "The Snoz" Grubberman, part-time supersleuth and ace food critic for the *Carnarsie Clarion*.
—*Don Stacom*
Rowayton, Connecticut

The aquarium had been shattered by a bullet, Red Cunio noticed as his feet squished on the sodden carpet, and the bullet hadn't been fired long ago, Red Cunio also noticed because the tropical fish, including a large angelfish, were still flopping around on the draining gravel at the bottom of what used to be an expensive aquarium, complete with ferns and an undergravel filter.
—*Michael Huttlinger*
Pacific Grove, California

Little could Phoenix O'Hara, Omaha's leading private eye, ever dream as he slid out of the sack that February Wednesday in his usual "morning-after" state of mind what a stacked deck that fascinating city on the Muddy Mo would be dealing from that day.
—*Marion Gregg,*
Larry Gregg
Riverton, Illinois

Bunny Berryman belied his name; he was a sour cop with a sour disposition and a face like two-week-old milk forgotten on the back porch step, and he knew it—he also knew his mother had given him a better name than Bunny, but he'd been called Bunny for so long he'd forgotten exactly what it was.
—*J. Thompson*
Rochester, New Hampshire

A hesitant trickle of blood eased down the forehead, boldly traversed the nose, paused to gain strength on the upper lip, and dove for safety to the capacious cleavage of Kip Agabashian's former client.
—*Robert Schmiel*
Calgary, Alberta, Canada

To say that she was beautiful would be so inadequate as to constitute damnation by faint praise; to say that she was dead, her once-lovely neck snapped like a twig in the hands of some rampaging Goliath, would be to state the appallingly obvious; to say that the gendarmes of the Twenty-first Precinct were curious as to how her nude body got into my bed would be this year's contender for understatement of the decade (I was rather curious myself, having never seen her before in my life, but knowing at a single glance that she was my kid sister).

> —*Art Hill*
> *Stoughton, Wisconsin*

I had just docked the Four Flusher at the marina in Saint Pete when this frosty, washed-out blonde came waltzing down the dock, batted her mink eyelashes demurely, and told me she was desperately in need of my services.　—*Thomas Whissen*
> *Dayton, Ohio*

MODERN LOVE

HELL HATH NO FURY . . .

"For such as believe that Love is and ought to be omnipotent, the following 'tale' can have but little attraction; and, on the other hand, to those, the unmercifully virtuous, who deem that to 'feel tempted, is to sin,' and who in their notions of the perfectable capacities of human nature, go beyond Pythagoras and Plato, it will have still less: for to them, the many-languaged voice of the passions is the unknown tongue of St. Paul, requiring interpretation; they are indeed 'righteous over much,' yet wanting all
  'The fair humanities of old religion.' "
    —Lady Lytton Bulwer,
      Cheveley; or, the Man of Honour (1839)*

* This novel by Bulwer-Lytton's wife is a roman à clef with a villain modeled after him. Their marriage was bitterly opposed by Bulwer-Lytton's mother, who temporarily disinherited him. She turned out to be right: Bulwer-Lytton and his wife were eventually separated, his wife spent some time in an asylum, and she devoted the remainder of her life to plaguing her husband's existence.

XXXXXXXXXXXXXXXXXXXXXXXXXXXXXXXXXX

Toilet bowl rims, not microchips, were the working domain of custodian Bob Johnson, and yet he had been astute enough to salvage that key piece of software from the trash, and standing in the window of the seventy-fifth-floor penthouse suite, he realized that his too-good dream of reward had become reality; the heart

of Rita Payne-Webbar, beautiful heiress to millions and brilliant twenty-four-year-old senior vice-president of Software Conglomerate International, was his. (from *Software, Hard Hearts*)
—*Jim Lovering*
Webster, South Dakota

The conjunction of a hangover, that lunar-synchronous spot of unpleasantness that Woman is heir to, and a bout of stomach trouble that would have cleared the dysentery ward at Delhi General made Ophelia's wedding night less romantic than she had always imagined it would be. —*Rex De Winton*
Bristol, England

After a long kiss, her nostrils flaring both from passion and from lack of oxygen, Velma pulled back slowly from Lloyd and, with her violet eyes ablaze, her quivering moist lips slightly parted, her breasts, firm as Delicious apples, heaving convulsively, she moaned, cracked her gum, and said, "Geez, I sure could go for a hamburger!" —*Lynn S. Black*
Massapequa, New York

Writhing in the elemental and furious rush of that scalding shower spray, Lucy thrilled to the memory of Jean-Luc's eager response handling and contour seats.
—*Terrence H. Seamon*
New Brunswick, New Jersey

The past several days had passed endlessly since the Screaming Eagle motorcycle gang rode into Maggie's life, leaving her studded with more excitement than she had ever known with

Stanley, yet exposing her to dreadful life-styles which shook the very foundations of her Southern Baptist upbringing.

—*Frank R. Adams III*
Pensacola, Florida

"Fightin' Joe" Steerforth thought he was tough until the day he met Annie ("Big Bucket") McGillicuddy and she left him battered and spent like a punch-drunk prizefighter on the ropes of love.

—*John Stark Bellamy II*
Cleveland Heights, Ohio

I was a rookie in the game of love, dropping a fly at the wrong time, mishandling the high, long ones, striking out at the plate; you see, my gentle word traveler, I couldn't tell if fair was foul or foul was fair.

—*Thomas O'Toole*
Knoxville, Tennessee

Every year on her return the ambience of this room never failed to move her deeply: the scent of the tuberoses wafting from the porcelain vase the solicitous management placed there for her delight, the ivory lace curtains aflutter in the French windows ajar to the balcony where she would sunbathe nude, framing Lac Lucerne where one white sail teetered crazily in the blue distance as in a Matisse painting; and, as she lifted the fluted crystal glass in her incredibly tapered fingers with their pearlescent nails, she abstractedly caressed the warm parquet floor with one matching lacquered bare toe as she took her morning's first sip of the Dom Perignon and turned her lithe torso toward him, secretly imagining what Lucinda, her grandmother's easily shocked factotum, would have said about this.

—*Alice Wirth Gray*
Berkeley, California

Ed McGuire was a big man, standing 6'4" in his red wool socks, and big-hearted as well, and he liked his women lean and tough, like hard-working bird dogs, trained to the gun and loving it.
—*J. Thompson*
Rochester, New Hampshire

One of the best things about her was her hair—a muted, sensuous auburn, like the color of dusky clouds in the western sky at sunset, tinged with a hint of red, and long and flowing like a meandering stream drifting lazily around the hillocks and mounds of an otherwise unremarkable landscape—and when she bent forward, her hair mercifully covered one of the worst things about her . . .
—*George H. Shands*
Madison, Wisconsin

Mary Jane turned her wedding band to the left and her hand to the right and her eyes straight upward, and then she said a roundabout prayer for her jumbled-up marriage, which had just gone down the drain.
—*H. Eugene Craig*
Atlanta, Georgia

In the rearview mirror she caught the cabdriver looking at her, and his eyes were molasses-dark and sweet, such eyes as she always saw in the increasingly frequent erotic dreams caused by a too-long period of postdivorce celibacy.

—*Julia Buonocore*
New York, New York

It was in our fulsome sixth month that she revealed to me her nymphomania, a revelation my mind's eye never ceases to evoke, sometimes through languorous mists, at others via turgid thun-

derstorms—which in any case I have come to think of as the happiest moment in my life. —*Larry Bennett*
Chicago, Illinois

Nine dust-breathing, eye-burning days on the road and Spike Murphy was finally pulling his overworked rig and his under-washed body into his resurfaced driveway, when he spotted the adulterous caresses of his big wife and her lover/brother-in-law in the second-floor bedroom window; she turned at the screeching of the air-braking sixteen-wheeler, their eyes met, and for the first time since Easter Mike could see that fiery furnace of passion, that unquenched thirst of lust, and that sexual vitality of a Big Ten coed in his wife's piercing sapphire eyes.
—*Alan Klehr*
San Francisco, California

During an exuberant rainfall, a languid bottle of salad dressing sat passively on a Formica countertop as her lips crushed satisfactorily against the velour upper railing of his mustache.
—*Jerry Mikorenda*
Huntington Station, New York

LYTTONY II

AND AMERICA ITS STICKS . . .

"In one of those green woods which belong so peculiarly to our island (for the Continent has its forests but England its woods) there lived, a short time ago, a charming little fairy called Nymphalin."
—opening sentence of
The Pilgrims of the Rhine (1834)

The sun oozed over the horizon, shoved aside darkness, crept along the greensward, and, with sickly fingers, pushed through the castle window, revealing the pillaged princess, hand at throat, crown asunder, gaping in frenzied horror at the sated, sodden amphibian lying beside her, disbelieving the magnitude of the toad's deception, screaming madly, "You lied!"
—*Barbara C. Kroll*
Kennett Square, Pennsylvania

The ship was sinking, its massive hull angling serenely down, sucking ripples of frothy currents over the bow, sighing almost as it gave its great heart to the illimitable depths, Marvin thought, though he didn't live to tell it.　　　—*Sharon V. Brown*
Los Gatos, California

"It was like fifty minutes of Hiroshima," Dr. Landis Adler-Gruber was to write to MJM studios three years later, but at the present it was merely the first session in the psychoanalysis of an ordinary housewife who docilely began to tell the good doctor

that though her life was going fine, she sometimes "felt like the devil," an ironic understatement if there ever was one.
—John Paul Vancini
Brooklyn Center, Minnesota

Dressed like frogs, the elite men of the Sabotage Section (SS) of the Upper Peninsula Separatists (UPS) silently stroked their way through the clammy cold of the numbing night waters of the Straits of Mackinac, their charges having been ingeniously and insidiously set to be detonated by the heavy tread of the governor of the enslaving state of Michigan to the south as he crossed the bridge in a few hours on his yearly Labor Day symbolic march north, the web-footed men anticipating eagerly the explosion that would blow the bridge and return their land to its independent isolation, to its natural atmosphere of bears, porcupines, ghost towns, and the wholesome trouserborne dumplings called pasties; the Big Mack Attack was on.
—Brian Deatrick
Hell, Michigan

There was Swiizma, the One, who in Funtinma was called Consofliposter, and in the mountains of Ottoman was called Canolopi, and in the deserts of Niestad was called Chizmana, but in Armoire it came to pass that He, the Almighty, the Majestic, the All-Powerful, was not called anything at all, truly, precisely, verily, actually, maybe, possibly because no one there had ever heard of Him.
—Mary K. Bradford
Daly City, California

"Ah, Maud[e], you milk-white fawn!"
—Alfred Lord Tennyson

Lady Maude listened vaguely to a buck alligator grunting its repulsive love call from the fetid ooze of the nearby tropical swamp and, as she gagged down three fat fingers of gin from the filthy tumbler in which Geoffrey's forgotten dentures still reposed, she wondered if he would ever return, wondered if he had ever loved her, wondered why she had so abjectly surrendered to the shabby triumvirate of Geoffrey, gin, and the jungle, wondered at the whole bloody eternality of it all, wondered if she'd have the guts to self-destruct before the gin was gone.
—*R. A. Macleod*
New Hartford, Connecticut

Although my father had told me that marvelous and strange things might happen when I least expected them, and when I might be least prepared for their appearance, I was left speechless—totally overwhelmed—by Dr. Reinhart's announcement, in front of the senior class (Maude, too) that my research project had been accepted by the university and that as a result I was being sent into isolation on a South Seas island—unnamed—to prove my thesis or die trying.
—*Hinda R. Miller*
Rochester, New York

There was a certain mysterious presence to Aunt Maude; she did nothing but sit in front of the television for days on end and then, one Thursday night, we discovered she was dead and had been dead so long she had mummified; and then we understood why we always watched the same channel week after week after dreary week.
—*M. S. Maire*
Cohasset, Massachusetts

David's lungs shuddered with spasms of pain but he kept going as the creepers and vines clutched at his flying feet, while in the clearing stood Felsted Abbey and the hellish shape that waited for him at the end of the hunt with bristling fur, razor teeth, and the satanic, near-human eyes of a dedicated lycanthrope.

—*Daniel Rich*
Fort Lee, New Jersey

All through her uneventful years as governess of the little Lord Fauntleroy, whose life story has been the subject of an excellent book that did not fail subtly to influence the upbringing of innumerable scions of the English nobility, keen as their parents were to keep up with the latest fashion, be it in education or in deep-sea fishing, as the Duchess of Malfi was prompt to remind me at the last party given by that poor Leonard who, a few days later, committed suicide, by a surfeit of caviar, on account of some ballerina, Miss Littleton has always prided herself on the integrity of her character, the single-mindedness of her devotion to her charge, and the clarity of her style.

—*Henry Bourgeot*
Lycée Français de La Marsa, Tunisia

With one final, fearsome paroxysm, the gargantuan tectonic plates converging below the former ocean bed under Sir Niles's recently—and quite tastefully—redecorated flat, exploded, forcing the ragged, wind-lashed mountain visible from the study window to totter and collapse, distracting Sir Niles as he drafted a hasty note to his man Fulton regarding the mysterious disappearance of his jogging shoes, so that he failed to hear Euphemia enter the room, gun in hand.   —*Bob Forrest*
Phoenix, Arizona

"Gainsay me no vainglory," vouchsafed the scapegrace, brusquely brushing past the craven varlet attending his steed, and, so averring, vaulted into the saddle and cantered insouciantly into the darkling copse, leaving Lady Llewyllen swooning with the vapors. —*Jack Tucker*
Berkeley, California

The veins in his huge, pulsing neck were more than Elizabeth's moral standards could bear, and she sucked, with great abandon, her breath in, whispering hoarsely, "Oh yes, Rose, yes, yes, yes." —*Lucinda L. Ryan*
Alameda, California

As she writhed and moaned, "No, no, no, no, no," he was "writhing" too, and hithing, "Yeth, yeth, yeth, yeth, yeth!" —*Laura-May Azpiazu Howley*
Hawaii Kai, Hawaii

"*Mein Gott*, I'm feeling so blue," mused *der Führer* as the bombs began belching beyond the moon-bright bunker. (from *A Callow Youth's Rhineland*) —*Webb Marris*
Pacific Palisades, California

OUR MAN
IN THE
VATICAN

IN SHORT, NOT A MAN
TO LOSE HIS HEAD

"In an apartment at Paris, one morning during the Reign of Terror, a man, whose age might be somewhat under thirty, sat before a table covered with papers, arranged and labeled with the methodical precision of a mind fond of order and habituated to business."

—opening sentence of
Lucretia; or, the Children of the Night (1846)

A sharp-pointed wing-tipped brogan hit me in the crotch—POW!—and it hurt real bad but Bobby Joelvitch Korisov the KGB agent had no idea he had tangled with Sister Theresa, disguised as a man, representing VESPER (Vatican Expeditionary Secret Police and Elite Religionists) so I just laughed—HA, HA!—and kicked *him* in the crotch with my black low-heeled Gucci health shoe, and watched with amusement as the Commie chauvinist pig scuttled off in a very low crouch.

—Bob F. Bledsoe
Richardson, Texas

Stealthfully as I slunk my slender fingers into the sleeping seaman's navy middy blouse pocket, the rustling of the corrugated cardboard on which was scrawled THE CODE caused his eyelids to flip open and his swarthy, swollen, brine-stained paws to enwrap my slim waist in a bear-clawed vise, whilst crying out loud, "Oh, it's you!" and throwing me over to fall upon me with pantherlike precision, bruising the twin buttercups of my bosom

and deflowering my frail beauty coarsely, enabling me to carry on my quest during his sweaty preoccupation with his goal baser than my own lofty one to save the nation. *—Patricia Dinnen*
Des Moines, Iowa

It came to him in a cocaine rush as he took the Langley exit that if Aldrich had told Filipov about Hancock only Tulfengian could have known that the photograph which Wagner had shown to Maximov on the jolting S-bahn was not the photograph of Kessler that Bradford had found at the dark, sinister house in the Schillerstrasse the day that Straub told Percival that the man on the bridge had not been Aksakov but Paustovsky, which meant that it was not Kleist but Kruger that Cherensky had met in the bleak, wintry Grunewald and that, therefore, only Frau Epp could have known that Muller had followed Droysen to the steamy, aromatic café in the Beethovenstrasse where he told Buerger that Todorov had known since the Liebermann affair that McIntyre had not met Stoltz at the Görlitzer Bahnhof but instead had met Sommer at the cavernous Anhalter Bahnhof.

—Richard Winkler
Brighton, England
Winner, Spy Fiction category

The rain's nasty, persistent clanging upon the roof of the sheet metal lean-to sounded not unlike a discordant drum solo in some crude and unfathomable rock anthem, mused Dexter O'Shaugh-

nessey, the gnarled and wizened ex-KGB killer turned Louisiana beet farmer, as he raced merrily about the decrepit little shack astride the leather saddle of "Big Mo," his rusted but faithful unicycle.   —*Don Stacom*
                                                      Rowayton, Connecticut

Shrouded in secrecy, cloaked in mystery, covered by a web of deception and murder, Rodney Groper (known to many only as "The Swallow!") pursued his elusive quarry—Bovadikov ("The Assassin!")—seen by many, survived by none, this ruthless exterminator who preyed on those who, for reasons too strange and varied to comprehend, found themselves drawn, as a moth to a flame, to this deadly predator who used as his method of execution that seemingly most innocent of devices, the acoustic guitar!
                                                      —*Ron Randolph*
                                                      Orange, New Jersey

"I must have been in this business too long—my nerves are getting shot," thought master spy Rockne Gates as he replaced his .357 Magnum in its holster behind his left knee, from which he had pulled it exactly .58 seconds after a child fired a cap pistol in the department store where Gates was buying a toy panda for his niece's third birthday.   —*Blair Hoffman*
                                                      Moraga, California

Rose was in a thorny situation; on the one hand she was stuck upon the notion to keep secret the coded message forwarded by the Nazi high command, which would trigger the annihilation of her village, while on the other hand her knotty love affair with Colonel Klanse transcended any loyalty to the people who had raised her as one of their own.   —*Frank R. Adams III*
                                                      Pensacola, Florida

Looking into the inscrutability of his hooded eyes, eyes sated, spaced out as deep pools of midnight, knowing that she had plumbed and salved the agony of his need, a need that had touched the very core of her being—Agent Agnes Propst suddenly realized that she had blown her cover.

—*Carl A. Kerr*
Glenville, West Virginia

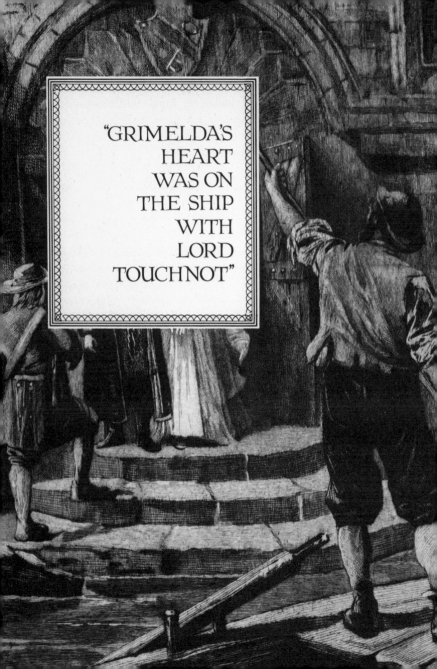

"GRIMELDA'S
HEART
WAS ON
THE SHIP
WITH
LORD
TOUCHNOT"

IS CONSTANCE CALM, KNIGHT?

"Is the night calm, Constance?"

—opening sentence of
Godolphin (1833)

Grimelda's heart was on the ship with Lord Touchnot, but her feet were planted firmly in the soil of her native land; she felt she could not endure the pain.
—*Mary Virginia Brown
Ventura, California*

As soon as the passions of the sudden summer storm had subsided, Désirée, tossing her raven hair and darting a fiery look of defiance at the cold, gray manor house, mounted her horse in one fluid motion and, gripping firmly with her thighs, whipped her stallion, bareback, across the steaming fields towards the sea, where the surf assaulted the cliffs relentlessly. (from *Flaming Inferno of Love*)
—*Nancy Heifferon
San Jose, California*

As she saw Thornecrest for the first time—high, forbidding, shrouded by storm—Dawn clutched to her trembling bosom the reticule containing the keys to this new, strange place, her application as governess, a hatpin smeared with curare, a locket containing the first joint of her mother's left little finger, the results of Lord Thorne's most recent Wassermann, and a small Baggie containing the last of the bread crumbs she had been dropping steadily since leaving Bog Farm.
—*Alan Becker
Colusa, California*

As Chastity Bannon stared stubbornly into the mirror, critically scrutinizing her tousled auburn hair, emerald-green eyes, and spirited mouth, she reflected upon her meeting with the handsome, mysterious, yet somehow brutal Derrick Trevellyan, lord of brooding Hardgate Castle.   —*Elaine K. Whitehouse*
New York, New York

As the sun sank slowly in the rolling bosom of the empurpled western hills and the stellar sentinels of night proclaimed the imminent arrival of their lunar mistress on the eastern horizon, Raoul Devereux sprang from his couch and strode to the balcony, flickering embers of his passion for the Lady Angela Tewkesbury already making incandescent his anticipation of their clandestine midnight tryst in the encircling rose-covered walls of the gazebo.   —*Laura Ferguson*
Salem, Oregon

Slowly, Vanessa became blindingly aware of his hot, steamy lips pressed tightly against her own delicate mouth, sending thrilling shivers throughout her young, eager body whilst the resounding warnings of her dear departed mother echoed in her ears—but she pushed them back into the further reaches of her mind, opening her heart, along with her sweet young lips, to Raoul's insistent pursuit.   —*Nancy L. Henry*
Rutherford, New Jersey

Out on the headland the billowing sea roared and thundered at her feet, while behind her the wind moaned, crickets chirped, bees buzzed, crows cawed and the leaves on the trees rustled and hissed like thousands of tiny whisperers; but, Lorna, in her blue velvet three-buttoned cape, trimmed in ermine and complemented by knee-high brown suede boots with matching gloves, was aware of none of it: her mind was on Brett.

> —*David Kenway*
> *Juneau, Alaska*

A rosy dawn crept over the hills like the scarlet flush on the bosom of the earth, which shone redolently with a pearly musk infusing all nature with its aroma, particularly the fringed gentians nodding against the great chimney of Broderick Hall, where the master and his household, in the panoply of a grand style long forgotten, savored the luxury of their circumstances without any knowledge or apprehension that the claret, by foul means unbeknownst to any but the wizened brain of the nefarious steward, had been laced with poison so offensive it could blacken their countenances by setting sun, and, as surely as shadows will fall when the sun rises, unless there is nothing to obstruct its rays, when they quaffed it, it did precisely that.

> —*Robert W. Shields*
> *Dayton, Washington*
> *Winner, Gothic Romance category*

The eerie reverberation of that chilling scream, piercing the gray fog like a steam-driven whistle, hardly audible here but of incalculable intensity at the point of origin, told a story of vapid horror and gross desires, yet was not without a human element, a romantic warmth that cannot be artificially created.

> —*V. Brown*
> *Quispamsis, New Brunswick, Canada*

Even the raging wind of the wild November night could not compete with the turbulence of Everard's mind as he lay tossing in his great ancestral bed, tormented by the glittering image of Juniper, dancing as no one had ever before danced in that stately ballroom, the brilliance of her eyes mocking the other women's diamonds, her siren smile penetrating him with its lure, as he had stood paralyzed, staring at this diaphanous apparition, unconscious of the social whirl, the tempting canapés, the antique fountain foaming with pink champagne.   —*The Watchetts*
Reading, England

She flung her feverishly disquieted body onto the cool cambric of the Waldorf-Astoria bed and knew, oh yes, sobbingly knew that her love was lost, so irrewinnably lost that her pearly teeth, absentheartedly in a sense, began gnawing the silky pillow her golden dreams had so lavishly blossomed on.   —*G. E. E. Simon*
Winterberg, West Germany
Winner, Romance category

Lady Muriel Willoughby-Gore looked misty-eyed across the once lovely, long-neglected drawing room of Gore–Saint Mary's and realized with dreadful certainty that—she was the failed end of a once proud line—she had failed in her duty as a wife, a mother, and a nurse—redemption was now beyond her—death was stalking her through the house like a cat after a rat—the dashing, charming, madly rich Julian Cassell was a Jew and her worldly salvation might also be her social demise.

—*Donald C. Cameron*
South Laguna, California

Pandora's bored gaze swept the ballroom, over the clusters of cavalrymen resplendent in their gold-braided, red uniforms, their shiny boots reflecting the twinkling glass chandeliers, past the fierce stare of a tall stranger on crutches, and back to his compelling, dark-lashed blue eyes the shade of a Tahitian lagoon in which she was drowning, cursing her father, a syphilitic nobleman, who had never taught her to swim.

—*Noriko Sawada*
San Francisco, California

Dace Branwell's eyes—eyes that held forbidden promises, hopes, dreams, eyes hard and brittle and bright as all outdoors, eyes that kept women and flung them away like empty beer bottles, eyes wise with winsome laughter yet retaining the darker strains of mystery under their furrowing brows—now swept their azure clearness from his feet to soar like two hawks to the very peak of Challenger Mountain, where they hesitated but a moment, relishing the contest pitting his brawn against the wilderness and the snowcapped peak, and then dropped quickly back down the green mountain, dancing and tumbling their way like merry boys keen in anticipation till they came to rest against the small but comfortable cabin, behind the oak door of which was golden-haired Dossey, the only woman man enough to bring Dace to bay.

—*Larry R. Isitt*
Coeur d'Alene, Idaho

Selwyn, the plain but sloe-eyed slim governess, stood shivering, clutching to her homespun cape, the exact color of Highland heather, which neatly matched her lavender eyes, high on a cliff in Cornwall above the sweeping moors, looking down at the storm-swept sea, thinking of Little Felicity, her petulant flaxen-haired charge, and wondering what was to become of her.

—*Ellen Antill*
Honolulu, Hawaii

No, her name was not Jeanie, but from his vantage-point he could see that her hair was light brown and, yes, it veritably did seem to float like a zephyr on the soft summer air—for indeed there was a gentle breeze, and it was summertime, and her hair was long and loose—and he found himself fantasizing that he was near enough for his face to be brushed in ever so featherly a fashion by wisps of that hair.   —*Dorothy W. Conner*
Fort Wayne, Indiana

Di knew as soon as she walked into the spacious, ornately furnished family room that Charles's parents, Beth and Phil, would never fully accept her as their daughter-in-law, but she loved Charles as she had never loved anyone and she was determined to become his wife and fulfill the promise the gypsy fortune-teller had made to her dying mother long ago in that sanitarium where she was born and lived for all those agonizing years until the doctor adopted her and took her home to the one woman he hated to deceive.   —*Anne L. Fairley*
Winnipeg, Manitoba, Canada

J. Holden Devereaux's plantation empire remained intact, even after the murderous Yankee troopers stormed Georgia, right down to the beautiful slave they called the Mulatto, the one who knew him even better than did his nymphomaniacal wife.

—*Steve Garman*
Pensacola, Florida

For three decades the last surviving members of the de Cheveaux clan had been meeting each year on February 29 at the family estate, Turnbridge-at-Drawbridge, where they dined on spotted dog and cream pickles, waded in the lily pond, and examined the outstanding collection of fifteenth-century jeweled toupee combs assembled by their ancestor, Rholande the Bald, first Viscount of Drawbridge. —*Leslie Rowena Pugh*
Berkeley, California

Blade leaned casually, elegantly, knife-slim, against the grand piano, his cruel slash of a mouth twisted with contempt as he gazed across the room at Peony, huddled in a soft mass in an overstuffed chair, her golden ringlets tumbling sensually, her bee-stung mouth pouting with pique as she listened to the harsh words issuing from the thin, carmined lips of Hester, words to the effect that neither Blade nor Peony could hope to inherit from the will soon to be read of Percy Hepplewith III, dead but not buried, who had confided to Hester that he was going to leave his fortune to his lover, Billy Quick, the gardener's son.
  —*Patricia A. McQuade*
Hoquiam, Washington

Silence reigned as the beautiful, albeit profound, Jennifer, with stealth born of desperation, slipped like a wraith into the cellar of the old abandoned mansion, which had been left to stand in all its ghostly magnificence since the murder of the last known heir of Glynnthorne. —*Carol Ann Webb*
Atlanta, Georgia

Her girlish "Oh no!" was still echoing through the half-open or carelessly semishut doors of the nobly renovated sixteenth-century forty-five-room castle as the aging earl nervously tried to

light a cigarette under the knowing looks of Mrs. Colleroy, the housekeeper, who had long before given up counting the skeletons in the cupboards whose flawless order she would never stop being honestly devoted to.   —*G. E. E. Simon*
Winterberg, West Germany

When Lucy Stovall first saw Heeber Forsythe riding by on the road that bordered her father's plantation, he was riding a black water-smooth stallion so naturally and so well that she knew how the Helots of ancient Greece, seeing men on horseback for the first time, could construe the sight as one animal, and she knew, had known, even then, that should he ever take notice of her, approach her, press her, say in some corner of the garden at dusk, with the fragrance of the honeysuckle refusing to stop, and finally propose to do what so desperately needed to be done, that the heavy walls of her restraint might crumble and finally, eternally, never-endingly her heart going like mad under the privet, yes, she would say to him, yes, yes, yes—or maybe, knowing as she, and only she, did, that her father and his were one and the same man.   —*Gene Ellis*
Atlanta, Georgia

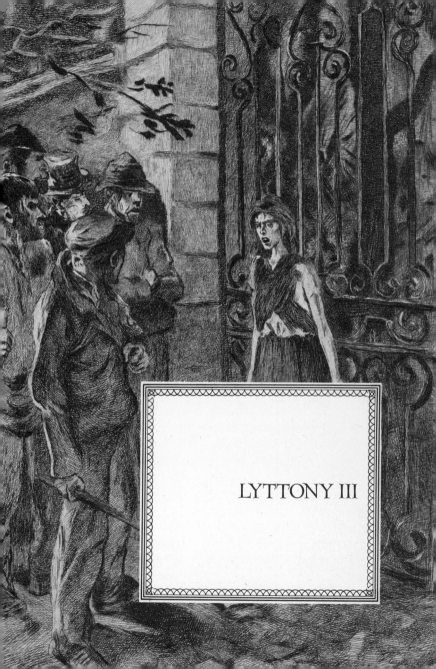

LYTTONY III

OK, SO THERE WAS A SMOG ALERT!

"It was a bright day in the early spring of 1869."
—opening sentence of
The Parisians (1872)

⁂

Elmer and Ernest, Siamese twins joined at the head since birth, sat eagerly awaiting their first roller coaster ride at the park.
—*Anita Barry*
North Hollywood, California

"Où est la guerre?" cried Captain Lance Jackson of Waco, Texas, as he leapt off his M4 Sherman Medium tank, his sharpshooting M1 carbine at the ready, to Lisette, the buxom young French farm girl, who murmured huskily in reply, *"Ah, mon brave, les boches sont finis ici."*
—*Edward C. Tannen*
Jacksonville, Florida

"Vous êtes très formidable," she purred, and I knew right then I should keep my eyes and ears open and my hands and nose and throat clean.
—*William MacKendree*
Paris, France

Bloodhounds bayed their triumph, a fishing pole tangled in an overhanging branch, and skid marks showed on the slippery rock below but, while the posse was dragging the raging torrent, the far-in-the-future Senator Dillworth lay shivering atop the caboose of an eastbound Norfolk and Western freight.

—*Eileen King*
San Francisco, California

The flames flicked quietly in a straight path toward the living quarters in the White House, while Fritz (Sandy) Renquist, second secretary at the U.S. embassy in Bombay, was losing a one-way fight with sleep aboard Trans-Pacific Flight 367 as it bored its way through the icy night air five miles above the roiling sea.

—*Namron Nosleba*
Concord, New Hampshire

The sky above the refineries was dwindling to a faded terra-cotta as the street urchin seized the stranger's hand and led him without protest to the small enclosed garden redolent of a burgeoning tropical paradise.

—*Carol Ann Webb*
Atlanta, Georgia

Dianne, the chief investigator of the ongoing multicultural, polycharacteristic, in-depth, and individualized psychological character analysis team, was dazzlingly beautiful in the classically cut, yet stylishly elegant blazer and pants ensemble with French overtones and Quaker-style lace trimmings, as she stepped off the Manhattan bus onto the dirty sidewalk.

—*Anthony Rosler*
Elsternwick, Victoria, Australia

"Well, we shall see, Madame Cherout," said Humphrey Hooke sardonically, defiantly, "if indeed you shall have your way

in this matter or if my considerable skills as a locksmith, learned in the service of the queen on the high seas and in the jungles of Borneo, shall stand me in good stead," his shackled hands crossing behind his back to conceal a small file, which he rubbed slowly, patiently, imperceptibly, back and forth on the chains which bound him, as his trusty owl Squire, caged just above his head, hooted softly, hauntingly, six times. —*Reloy Garcia*
Omaha, Nebraska

She had thought that something like a blintz did not matter in this war-torn world of 1918 and that cooking, nor any of the normal activities normally undertaken by her, Adele Micrandon del Purifoy, would ever be the same again, war or no war, and so in spite of herself she lunged at the last strawberry blintz and, like a hidden land mine, it exploded in her face, a face that Frank would, even now, be traveling 16,000 miles to see from his billet in the south of France, and he would forget Mimi, the student nurse; and Jacque, the Apache dancer; and Lois, the real estate speculator; and all that crazy lost generation and they would be married . . . or so she thought. (from *Something Like a Blintz*)
—*W. Joseph Hartnett*
Santa Monica, California

When the whole town congregated to discuss (as they often do in smallish towns) what moniker to bestow upon Blanche McCoy's out-of-wedlock baby girl, little did they know, in choosing the name *Blondine* (pronounced *Blan-deen*), that, blossomed into womanhood some years later, her name would suit her to a proverbial T as she spent her many idle hours unobtrusively draped in her gray terry-cloth wraparound (that exactly matched her walls) contemplating with furrowed brow upon such profundities as supermarket mark-ups, soiled sea gulls, and vegetarian mulligan stew—among other myriad matters of life's complexities—and thus, gentle reader, her entire timorous life will be fully explored in the ensuing chapters, which were written and designed for your total reading pleasure.

—*Joan Scott*
Slaterville Springs, New York

Once upon a time, a very very very *long* time ago (*ever* so long ago), a teeny tiny weeny furry bear (smaller than most) named Norbert Smythe lived with a great many other teeny tiny weeny furry bears in a cozy cave lined with cupboards filled with honey jars and jam tarts and other yummy gooey treats fixed by Norbert's mummy (who loved him just as much as your mummy loves you and always tucked him into his teeny tiny weeny furry bed each night and dressed him each morning in little blue coveralls and a red and white striped jersey and a cunning little sailor hat) in the middle, the absolute center, of a great big huge *enormous* forest and lots of bunnies and squirrels and mice and ducks and quite a few lambs and puppies and just a few kittens lived just around the corner so Norbert had ever so many exciting adventures and all-round fun times; this is the story of just *one* of those all-round fun times and if you like this story, you can ask mummy and daddy to buy you all the rest of the forty-seven books in this series. —*Gail Cain*
San Francisco, California
Winner, Children's category

Ruby Jewel pranced back and forth across the corral, her long, sorrel mane and tail frothily floating behind her like an other-worldly afterglow, and then, her arched neck silhouetted against the salmon-pink dawn for one scintillating suspended second, she wheeled and trotted toward Timothy with a low, undulating whinny, thus signaling her farewell to the freedom of the open range of yore, and she nuzzled her velvety nose into his upturned palm, as with her soulful, chocolate-brown eyes she told him that she was his own, dear, equine princess at last.

—*Mary D. Edwards*
Oklahoma City, Oklahoma

Screaming like a banshee, bargaining like a waterfront drug dealer, bleeding like a side of beef in an abattoir, the Chinese sailor croaked out one word: "Firelight" (a code word? or a dying man's resurrection of a beloved childhood memory?) and fell to the ground, sprawled out like an electrocuted lobster, clutching in his fist loosened by the merciful kiss of death fire of another sort: a 20-carat, flawless blue diamond. —*Marilyn A. Thompson*
Galveston, Texas

THE WAY
WE LIVE
NOW

DOES HE MEAN HENRY OR HARRY?

"My grandfather, Sir Arthur Devereux (peace be with his ashes!) was a noble old knight and cavalier, possessed of a property sufficiently large to have maintained in full dignity half a dozen peers—such as peers have been since the days of the first James."　　—opening sentence of
Devereux (1829)

━━━━━━━━━━━━━━━━━━━━━━━━━━━━━

I mean, they were kind of mellow times, but not exactly state-of-the-art times, if you follow.　　—*Peter Schermerhorn*
Rochester, New York

"Totally grody to the max," murmured Patty as wimpy Max Grody slouched across the Valley through the dark, stormy night, grabbed her, and like, you know, gagged her with a spoon.
—*H. Winton Ellingsworth*
Tulsa, Oklahoma

It's pretty well known around this place that I'm single and am looking for a man with some pretty awesome megabucks—that's for sure!　　—*Scott Castillo*
San Jose, California

Her life rent asunder by the vicissitudes of traveling in the fast lane, Dee Dee, with a small brave smile, faced up to the herculean task of finally getting her head straight.　—*Dick Holt*
Chicago, Illinois

A whiff of smoke swirled around Joe's head, reentered his nostrils, smothered his eyes, flooded his tongue, and sank down deep into his throat, just as the first puff of marijuana is wont to do.
—*H. Eugene Craig*
Atlanta, Georgia

"Yes, *Paul Clifford* is my very favorite novel of all time, fur shur, I mean it's so totally AWESOME!" the beautiful young English lit professorship applicant gushed as she sat opposite the entranced, aging, old dean.
—*M. D. Lucas*
Fort Worth, Texas

You name it, I've seen it—the depths, the pits, the bottom; Vic Steele's the name, and proctology is my game.
—*William J. O'Malley, S.J.*
Rochester, New York

Stoney Glasshouse couldn't believe his eyes—you know, the cool, incandescent ones that sat smack dab in the middle of the face that had been splashed across the cover of every magazine that had, or thought it had, its finger on the pulse of contemporary modern culture—when he saw, or maybe it was a hallucination, his doppelgänger buying a pint of bruised strawberries.
—*Red Wassenich*
New York, New York

With the determination and rugged precision of an automatic log-splitter, Fanny, known by friends as Hercules and Bruiser, and by a select few as Snapper, with the profound depth of stealth approaching dizzying heights of epic proportions, crept his quivering hand into his mother's vaguely wet and slimy makeup case, where he espied the black and shiny, impeccably sawed-off instrument of pain he so desperately desired.

—*Paul Bayley*
Burlingame, California

Staring at the starkly white sheet of paper in his typewriter, John wondered—is it possible to write a novel, even the first *sentence* of a novel, in such a self-conscious and hyperreflective age?

—*John D. Glenn, Jr.*
New Orleans, Louisiana

The pot sweet Aunt Alice used to water her Appy gelding lay at Barney's feet filled with flopping bullheads he didn't even know how to skin, not if he was going to use those pliers instead of the great big nail Uncle Charlie had shown the other girls and me how to use in the shed, which he had driven all the way through the oak post and bent upwards before he died, the summer it had all begun for us.　　　—*Michael Sonnen*
Redlands, California

How little could I foresee, as I sat nervously awaiting the employment interviewer's seemingly endless perusal of my application for senior laundress to the House of Representatives, of my sixteen never-to-be-forgotten years of warmth, humor, and humanity to come in the corridors of power.

—*Simon B. Arnstein*
Baltimore, Maryland

The WASP conservative Republican clutched his copy of the *Moral Majority Newsletter* while sipping his decaffeinated coffee on the porch overlooking the flat Kansas land, while watching a Donahue program concerning the sexual habits of Mongolian gerbils inoculated with truth serum by the scientists from Columbia University College of Animal Husbandry.

—*Elizabeth Nieuwland*
Old Orchard Beach, Maine

Let me tell you how luck, hard work, blind ambition, and the love of a good woman brought Rock Sledge from obscurity to the job of chief salesperson in Peoria's third-largest shoe store.

—*Marion Gregg,*
Larry Gregg
Riverton, Illinois

Under the spasmodic neon sign of the No-Tell Motel, Dwayne Shiflett slouched contentedly in the fake-fur upholstery of his beloved Rambler American and aimlessly picked his teeth with his comb, his thoughts straying to that other object of his passion, the fry-cook Ramona at the Route 1 Weenie Beenie.

—*Laura Snow*
Alexandria, Virginia

I was a fifty-four-year-old male virgin but I'm all right now.

—*Arden Ohl*
Modesto, California

Over the top, jamming the Fuller Roadranger into Georgia overdrive, down the western slopes of the Rocky Mountains, into the curves, over the road, Slade Stomply slung the runaway behemoth of a truck, the vibrant throb of the life pulsing in his strong veins echoing in the throb of the stinking Chalmers diesel under the doghouse at his elbow, in the throb of the eighteen tires on the concrete surface of the interstate highway, in the throb of the traffic that coursed through the concrete arteries of the nation from one shining sea to the other.

—*Bill Burnette*
San Jose, California

FRITT FITT
WOPPIDY
WUPPIDY
CHICHU

YOU TRY IT IF YOU THINK
YOU CAN SPELL WELSH NAMES!

"In one of the Welsh counties is a small village called A——."
                                                    —opening sentence of
                                                    Night and Morning (1841)

━━━━━━━━━━━━━━━━━━━━━━━━━━━━━━━━━━

Fritt fitt woppidy wuppidy chichu . . . Xydu, explorer extraordinaire of the Great Green Star Cluster, knew from the sound and wrenching tossing of his spacecraft that the gyroscopic generator was failing fast, and he was over 42 light parcels from the civilized center of the universe, but Xydu knew no fear for no true warrior Chaga Bol Dar ever knew fear; yet a strange coldness he had never felt before touched the base of his spine and raced up his backbone when the fritt fitt woppidy wuppidy chichu came to an abrupt halt and the eerie silence of eternity filled Xydu's ears.
                                                    —*Marcia Mercer*
                                                    Ramona, California

Her writhing body sinewed under the physical strain, arching and throwing her full breasts upward; her perfectly rounded thighs, sparkled with a thin layer of sweat and forced wide open, struggled to close against the inanimate arms of the Nautilus machine.
                                                    —*Peter Lau*
                                                    Pasadena, California

Driven by Margaret's steady hand, the Kirby vacuum worked a familiar path through the richly appointed Wilson home, its beater-bar action pounding out a rhythmic drone, preventing her from hearing, not more than 200 feet away, the slow descent of a cigar-shaped spacecraft onto her freshly mowed back lawn, the eerie craft's searing exhaust frying the blue enamel of the family's station wagon into ominous pools of glowing vapor and popping metallic trash-can lids in cacophonous tribute.

—*Donald L. Barnhart*
Jekyll Island, Georgia

"The natives must be hibernating," said Xanthosnon to his flight companion, the lovely Zanthosnon, as they gazed at a group of scarecrows standing silhouetted against a bleak but windless autumn sky shortly after their star car, an XAN 12 WX, landed in a cornfield near Davenport, Iowa.

—*Blair Hoffman*
Moraga, California

It had been three days since Torfongu had eaten Los Angeles, and now he sat staring down at Bakersfield . . . a tasty little morsel indeed.

—*Patrick L. Shepard*
Eagan, Minnesota

Marshall Ringo caught a subtle glimpse of Amanda's passionate amber tresses (while coolly fingering his Colt .45) as he deduced the fact that the surreptitious Black Bart was actually R2-B2 from Xerol—because ole B.B. had let it slip when he spat out his challenge: "This planet's not big enough for the both of us!"

—*Chuck Hustedt*
Morgan Hill, California

Plgnthgr had hidden his mtskrthkl in the mothchenth, and now he had taken the beautiful and magical Mekthkn and her infant Trmyljp there, too, and they all trembled as they heard the fearful chtlems of the invading Hrnewrs just above.

—*Mary A. Harrison*
Marietta, Georgia

The aliens bent over backwards, literally, to please their visitors.

—*Jane Amanda Espenson*
Berkeley, California

The two astronauts huddled on the surface of the planet Hemorrh (whose inhabitants took their name from an endemic, loathsome ailment), frozen in horror as the vile, slimy monster made its way relentlessly through the dark and stormy night toward the shambles of their wrecked spacecraft, oblivious of the fusion-generated force field which grizzled old Dr. Zneff had boasted would stop even the charge of a giant Kadinga.

—*H. Winton Ellingsworth*
Tulsa, Oklahoma

Under an edible sky, cheesy as a deep-dish pizza, X examined his sister's blork.

—*Beloved Remington*
Newport Beach, California

Sarah Jane-Marie Jessica Amy Poinsdell-Updyke, or, as her friends called her, Rebecca Leigh Kathi, was the new Caffinotragent Officer on board the starship *Biloxi Bay,* and a lovelier yeoman—or a more curious—would be hard to find.

—*Paula Smith*
Kalamazoo, Michigan

"*Meteor storm!*" Sparks cried, almost throwing the professor's frail body against the bulkhead in zero-grav haste, ignoring Zor-

tran Threndoran's flailing purple tentacles in his fruitless effort to reach the null-space communicator as Bob Star slammed thruster levers into maximum and hoped against impossible odds that their shuddering, nearly fuelless Starcruiser would reach light-speed before the juggernautlike space rocks smashed them, along with the Federation's last hope for peace and Bob Star's only hope for real love, the professor's beautiful daughter Diana, into the cold oblivion of deep space.   —*Mike Montgomery*
Farmington, New Mexico

Long waves of emotional outcry floated down the metal flume Jason called his spinal column; his synthetic intelligence, packed tightly in microfine circuits within an alloy-based cranium logically placed below his left pivotal armpit, worked overtime impulsing signals representing frustration and rage from a matrix of zittermium connectors to sensor facial wires underneath near-human skin.   —*Stephen L. Gillies*
Norman, Oklahoma

The fourteen moons of Bbrasooforth whirled a dizzy minuet in the velvety dark skies of the Grashintooth Galaxy, but there was no warmth there to meet Ramshintoey's three Tyrian purple eyes except for the menacingly evil glint of the Hgrathindic Citadel where, on that fateful morning six Proklian revolutions before, the two-clawed Borks of Askar had solar-gunned the walls and torn his parents limb from web-footed limb.
—*Sharron Cohen*
Gloucester, Massachusetts

Beneath the third sun of Ur, the Earthmen, cautious after the disasters on ParII and WycomIV, came forth from their gleaming ship prepared to retreat at the slightest sign of hostility; but the natives (if such a flop-eared, one-eyed, hangdog group of aliens could be called native to anything) seemed friendly (albeit restless), and the air was the air of Earth, and the men were gradually relaxing, when it suddenly happened.

—*J. Thompson*
Rochester, New Hampshire

As Freeman's mind crawled oozily back into his skull like a blindworm from the mud planets of the Favath system, the sickening rubberiness of his limbs, which made him wonder for a moment if he had somehow traded bodies with his friend 'Mnen, proved that he had been subjected to a Belson probe field, and he knew from the streaks of slime on his face and bared chest, and the stench (even while the girl's traitorous farewell kiss still perfumed his lips), that it had been done at the hands, so to speak, of his old friends the Qatharxis; the alumiplast fingers of his own left hand strained vainly against his bonds to reach the contraband Federation-issue blaster pack, which in any case was no longer at his belt.   —*Robert Waltz*
Atlanta, Georgia

Red and green blood throbbed with passion unexpectedly between the little, greenish, three-toed humanoid emerging from the pulsating, silvery, cigar-shaped ship and the brown-skinned, feather-decked, six-shooter-toting Indian princess astride the dappled, earth-pawing, pinto pony.

—*Hilda Dennis*
West Palm Beach, Florida

By arching his shiny carapace and straining his antennae, the Zdont could just detect the last lappings of the waves of thin Ptonthlipian air heaved up by the huge arachnidesque machine,

which was even then settling onto the crusty surface of quadrant
zeta.
                                        —*Robert Schmiel*
                                        Calgary, Alberta, Canada

---

The surface of the strange, forbidden planet was
roughly textured and green, much like cottage cheese gets
way after the date on the lid says it is all right to buy it.
                                        —*Scott Davis Jones*
                                        Sausalito, California
                                        Winner, Sci-Fi category

---

I watched in helpless horror as the monster clawed its way up
the TV tower and wondered what could be in the mutated genes
of these Alaska king crabs which caused them to snatch only Canadian aircraft from the sky.
                                        —*Walter J. Murphy*
                                        Staten Island, New York

LYTTONY IV

THOUGH, AS YOU WILL SEE, THIS HAS ABSOLUTELY NOTHING TO DO WITH THE STORY

"I am an only child."
—opening sentence of
Pelham; or, the Adventures of a Gentleman (1828)

━━━━━━━━━━━━━━━━━━━━━━━━━━━━━

As the overcrowded steamship battled its way westward, ever westward, through frenzied seas towards America, the emigrant passengers, who had seen the last of Mother Ireland two days back when County Cork belied its name and sank in the ocean, huddled miserably below deck, each racked with painful memories of the past, anxiety about the future, and seasickness, but none more so than twenty-one-year-old Bridie O'Reilly, now two months pregnant after a chance meeting with a black evangelist in Sligo and more than a little apprehensive at the thought of joining Sean, her betrothed, who had staked out a beat for himself as a New York policeman this last Twelfth Night.

—*Kjell Yri*
Pokeno, New Zealand

As I sit here gazing at the pictures of those I once loved: Father and Aunt Cele entwined on the beach at Cap d'Antibes; Mother sipping sherry in the bathroom; Grandfather ducking into the Naughty-Nite Cinema; Lord Twillingham fishing for dimes in the Underground; Pamela "borrowing" a bracelet from Harrods; Rev. Dyson scorched from too many nights of chemin

de fer; Dr. Pomfret rewiring the respirator; and, of course, Colonel Bushcock and the lifeguard, I can't help but think there is a lesson to be learned from each and every one of their stories.
—*Larry Laiken*
New York, New York

As he wiped the mustard off of his sea-foam-green leisure suit, Rick Rome glanced through the café window and there, under the streetlight, stood Delores DuBois, murderess of his third wife, the late, lamented Wanda Whittier Rome.
—*Charles C. Rogers*
Ames, Iowa

As our eyes locked in a silent embrace across the crowded room, time stood still and I, tingling down to the very marrow of my bones, spasms racking my entire being, was delirious with the unchecked passion and wanton lust I felt for this total stranger whose hypnotic eyes hungrily devoured my trembling body— and, for the first time in my uneventful life, I understood the meaning of the word *fate*.
—*Lynda Correll*
Brick, New Jersey

As James drew, without inhaling, on his No. 1 special filter, a sixth sense that reached out from his distant hominid ancestor was sending stabbing signals through his cortex—could there be, was there not a half-seen shadow in the pall of darkness, a half-heard footfall in the hush of night . . . or were they tricks of light and sound sent to tease his jangled nerves?
—*Bill Nicoll*
Brussels, Belgium

> Muffy needed a new dress for the Big Dance, something expensive, something provocative, something grown-up enough to make her stand out from the other girls and catch the eye of Kip, the one boy in the world she wanted to notice her.
>
> —*J. Thompson*
> *Rochester, New Hampshire*

> It was a stark and dormy night, thought Muffy Veneris, a Latin major, as she sat in the empty hallway of the college residence that had not only housed her and her sisters, but had housed her dreams, aspirations, and a truly marvelous collection of fluffy stuffed animals which had once adorned her bed and shelves and the absence of which drove home to her the simple and frightening truth uttered to her by Dr. Landers just that morning which rang in her ears even now: "Muffy, not only did the rabbit die, but I think Nurse Hayes is coming down with something; Muffy, you're a woman now!"
>
> —*Steve Kronen*
> *Coconut Grove, California*

The fiery imprint of Wes Frontier's passionate kisses still burned on her hungry lips as Brittany Ireland watched the ruggedly handsome IRS agent stride determinedly from her bedroom.
　　　　　　　　　　　　　　　　　—*Pam Bardo*
　　　　　　　　　　　　　　　　　San Marino, California

Alone, now, for the very first time in what was to be *her* nursery, Prudence adjusted her stiffly starched nurse's cap and surveyed the thirty-six bassinets (yes! she had counted them!) where all the newborns lay sleeping, their nascent dreams gently swaying in their tiny heads like chiffon curtains in the breeze, and, when she did, an ineffable feeling of seemingly limitless altruism welled up in her bosom, causing her to declare—out loud, even—"My life's work has just begun!"

—*Mary D. Edwards*
Oklahoma City, Oklahoma

"L'amour, la mort," Jean-Paul said, pausing to flick the ash off the half-smoked Gauloise into the heavy, reeking ashtray, which overflowed angrily onto the yellow-lit plastic of the café tabletop, "it's all the same, all equally meaningless, all invalid as a response to . . . *comment le dire?* . . . empty questions."

—*Christopher J. Hickey*
Rabat, Morocco

I accessed the vehicle by upending the barrier that prevailed across the front of the facility, thus providing a way, approach-wise, to the automobile from two sides, one available to me, as I usually prevailed driver-wise, whereas my companion, in the case in point my spouse, preferred to occupy the seat adjacent to the driver's, where she was in an appropriate position to provide instructions as to route, destination, speed of passage, and to make such comments on my proficiency performance-wise as she deemed necessary and to prioritize most emphatically the most obvious deficiencies in my operation of our newly acquired automatic-shift four-wheel-drive vehicular facility, recently procured by us from a dealer in such automotive vehicles who gained access to such means of transportation from an importer with direct connections, procurement-wise, to a manufacturing facility located on the far shore of the Pacific Ocean, in the Empire of Japan.

—*Elbridge*
Granville, New York

"Airplanes fly slowly on Sundays," she pondered (misinterpreting the muted roar of lawn mowers), and soon she would discern that there is more in life than C-section scars and backgammon, and that the right man *will* haunt every chamber of the nautilus of her mind. —*Estella Kohler Leppert*
Tallahassee, Florida

IN DUBIOUS
TASTE

OR IS IT
"THE *VERBIAGE* GREW UP
IN SICKLY PATCHES"?

"Some four miles distant from one of our northern manufacturing towns, in the year 18——, was a wide and desolate common; a more dreary spot it is impossible to conceive—the herbiage grew up in sickly patches from the midst of black and stony soil."

—opening sentence of
Ernest Maltravers (1837)

Her eyes were a greenie-blue sort of, and reminded him of that exquisite passage in which Coleridge described a bowl of urine by moonlight.

—*Grovel P. Drivel*
Hollywood, California

In these uncertain times, one must think of others' viewpoints and always remember that a crowded elevator smells different to a midget.

—*Randy Irwin*
Winter Park, Florida

Flaherty sat there, playing with the bullet they'd dug from her body, like someone who'd picked his nose a lot as a kid.

—*Mike Snyder*
Hollywood, California

It all started on one of those usual mornings as I walked through Central Park with *The New York Times* over my head to protect me from the pigeons' small but significant bombs.

—*JoAnn Ricks*
San Jose, California

The sleeping woman grunted and turned over onto her side: "At least the snoring's stopped," mused Nigel, "but why am I so attractive to these hogs?"

—*Mary A. Harrison*
Marietta, Georgia

Alice fled to the ladies' room, locked herself into one of the stalls, and let out a huge sigh of relief.

—*Claude Clayton Smith*
Shawsville, Virginia

Heatherton stood menacingly at the very edge of the dark rampart, his formidable apelike figure starkly outlined against the nasty void by a sudden crack of lightning, and, amid the horrid din of growling thunder and precipitous downpour, shouted up at Emily, who hung limply in the belfry, her head almost severed by the taut, wet hangman's noose, "I say, woman, does this mean my supper will be late again?"

—*Hurd Hutchins*
New York, New York

The blue plastic fork produced a dull twang as Blodkin deftly propelled a greasy chunk of last night's hamburger from between his central incisors with one of the tines, and onto the distorted mirror, which shot back a warped image of his dark and gloomy face and the glint of gunmetal from his holstered .38.

—*Richard Clopton*
Alameda, California

Once upon a concussion in the blindest alley on Pender Street in the dope port of Vancouver, Creed Sheepwash woke up to the tune of the Led Zeppelin colliding with fifty rat-ass ash cans; he'd gone to bed with a succulent schoolmarm in Kitsilano and came to with a three-legged tomcat licking the blood from his broken nose.
—*Lost John Lyle*
Surrey, British Columbia, Canada

By the remorseless light above the operating table, which shone deep into the blood-washed cave of the open chest, hazel-eyed nurse Cynthia watched young Dr. Wilson's hands do their work on the heart, and in a sudden swell of passion she felt jealousy toward the patient.
—*Wolfgang Rumpelsberger*
Delafield, Wisconsin

That Matt Waco's horse was crippled was for sure but he couldn't reckon why pus was oozing from its skull.
—*Scott Davis Jones*
Sausalito, California

"Billingsley had been feeling rather down in the mouth due to the performance of the Dow Jones that week, combined with the lackadaisical behavior of his own personal portfolio," quoth the toothless, flea-bitten old whore, who had just regurgitated some tainted muscatel she had drunk out of an old rusty dog-food can, all over herself.
—*Marc L. Schnitzer*
Rio Piedras, Puerto Rico

She held it in her hands, gently rubbing the long, warm cylinder, its skin taut against the rich, full moisture of the inside and perfectly shaped yet smaller than the others she had gathered in the past hot month; her fingers massaged the soft, spongy tip—it

was satiated and rich, ready to open and burst white slime onto her fingers—she thought to put it in her mouth, but, no, a little too ripe, she thought and picked up the Chinese carving knife from the counter and chopped off the rotten end: "The zucchini season is almost over and, Frank my dear, I don't give a damn," she said to her husband who, startled, wide-eyed, looked up at her from over the rim of his coffee cup and stopped in midbite of his zucchini bread.   *—Pat Ramberg*
White Bear Lake, Minnesota

SUDDEN
TURNS

HAD WE BUT WORLD ENOUGH AND TIME, SENTENCES LIKE THIS WOULD BE NO CRIME!

"Westward, beyond the still pleasant, but, even then, no longer solitary, hamlet of Charing, a broad space, broken here and there by scattered houses and venerable pollards, in the early spring of 1467, presented the rural scene for the sports and pastimes of the inhabitants of Westminster and London."

—opening sentence of
The Last of the Barons (1843)

※※※※※※※※※※※※※※※※※※※※※※※※※※※※

As the unwanted baby made its demands upon her body and the pain of bringing this new life into the world consumed her consciousness, she breathed the words, "How did it happen?"

—*L. Mathews*
Bloomington, Minnesota

As the night flung itself onto the already storm-darkened land, out of the past came my mother's wavering voice, calling thinly, pitifully, "Sooooooooey! Suey, suey, sooooooooooey!!"

—*Carrie Geiger*
New Richmond, Wisconsin

As the giant ball of fire, illuminating the sleepy, serene countryside, hurtled from the nocturnal sky and plummeted into the

middle of the tiny hamlet of Broken Water, Maine, virtually destroying all forms of plant and animal life within a 25-mile radius and leaving nothing but a smoldering, searing inanimate path of destruction reminiscent of man's all-too-recent heinous sorties on Hiroshima and Nagasaki, Steve Jenne, from an overlooking mountaintop 30 miles away, excitedly turned to his fiancée and asked, *"Wow! Did you see that?"*   —*Stephen R. Jenne*
Springfield, Illinois

As he clenched his teeth in anger, muscles stood out along his jaw (at the sides where the lower jaw is nearest the ears, which in his case had not been cleaned in at least a week), their tension bringing the cords of his neck to such prominence that they bulged like steel cables of a size thick enough to hang a ski lift from; his eyes, close-set and piggish, flared icy fire as he glared at the sight before him, his tongue wagging furiously as he berated the petite, middle-aged clerk spreading out at the middle (a woman unattractive to most men, with graying hair and rhinestone-studded glasses, though he gladly would have bedded with her) unaware that with his next words he would set in motion a chain of inexorable circumstances that would plunge him into the lap of joy and into the black abyss of darkest despair: "What do you mean, you're out of Charmin?" he said.

—*W. Christian Lavallie*
Ithaca, New York

Priscella limped slowly, pensively, even a little bit painfully, out to the very water's edge, the dainty thump-thumping of her wooden leg now muffled by the thick fog swirling around her pathetically thin and misshapen form, shivering as it was inside a dirty threadbare sackcloth cape, and there she paused a moment, staring down at the cold, dark river rushing by, and thought to

herself, tears welling up in her sunken, feverish eyes: " 'To be or not to be, that is the question'—what groovy lyrics for my new rock oratorio!"
—*Hurd Hutchins*
New York, New York

Dick Straith may have been captain of the football team but why, he thought, should that stop him from wearing his sister's tube top.
—*Scott Davis Jones*
Sausalito, California

Maggie hesitated: abuse is no argument against its proper service in the cause of truth and right, yet to excite emotion in a man's mind is to sway his judgment, for the essence of it lies in the arguments or proof—could she warp his carpenter's rule?
—*Ann M. (Currah) Harvey*
New Brunswick, New Jersey

She seemed to have a theological halo around her head as she ambled towards him with that peculiarly sexy way of walking which was really due to an old spinal injury and incipient arthritis.
—*Jeanne-Marie Bonk*
Scotia, New York

He couldn't believe it, I mean, it simply wasn't possible that someone that lovely, that lithe and beautiful, so gentle and sensitive to his needs, his deepest inner masculine nature, could conceivably snore.
—*Stephen Mark Bartell*
Los Angeles, California

Unconsciously Delaney let his dirty fingers run over his pale, lank hair as, without regrets, he watched the tears well in the depths of Stephanie's amethystine eyes, her redeeming feature,

before coursing down the valleys that furrowed her tanned and now careworn face . . . the onions were almost ready.
—*Kim Mezdrum*
Macclesfield, Cheshire, England

I knew full well that I had checked, and rechecked, the appropriate box, yet an unmistakable feeling of sepulchral dread pervaded my very soul, reaching icy fingers of warning deep down into the farthest reaches of my shivering, desperate, racked, and quivering being; could I—though I almost dared not even think it—could I have checked "Female"?
—*Terrence H. Seamon*
New Brunswick, New Jersey

In the city of lost souls that was Los Angeles, the silvery halo above Kitty Gillis's head blinked a neon message to every two-bit grifter and pimp in sight: "I'm from Kansas, I'm alone, and I'm a virgin."
—*Scott A. Durfee*
Lewisville, Texas

The dark *can* be scary, thought Todd, if you're young, impressionable, intoxicated, out of gas, naked, and are forced to sit on vinyl seats.
—*Rix Quinn*
Fort Worth, Texas

The white-haired, grizzly-bearded old man sat center stage under the blue spot and softly fingered chords on his guitar until quiet descended on the crowd around the bar and, then, began his lament in a lonely wail:
H'yar in a 'Bama prison, on my lonely cot,
Larned life's greatest lesson: you cain't
Pound a nail in a knot!
—*Elaine Huegel*
Green Bay, Wisconsin

His expensive Brooks Brothers suit beginning to bulge uncomfortably through the middle, Jack walked slowly to the podium to deliver the annual Rotary Club lecture, and only then did he glance at the folder he had so carefully labeled "Speech" to discover it said "Acme Welding, Accounts Receivable."
— *Matteva Conmy Ahearn*
Edison, New Jersey

Just beyond the Narrows the river widens.
— *Warren Tupper Way*
Wayzata, Wisconsin

Her full, voluptuous mouth sensually lipped an invitation to excitement and passion while her cold, steely, piercing eyes unblinkingly turned aside any approach to familiarity or intimacy; or was it the other way around? — *Lawrence H. Zisman*
East Windsor, New Jersey

It was there, standing by the old well where poor Jennie died, that I felt the first efflorescence of coming manhood as from the Stygian depths of my milk-soaked childhood mind there arose— like a dance of little fishes—the atavistic diorama Jennie had innocently painted there, and although it remained for but a few moments, redolent with nostalgia, before sinking back down into the synaptic depths, it left me in a state of confused, albeit embarrassing, tumescence. — *John M. O'Keefe*
Tujunga, California

The sun cast an iridescent glow onto the oily surface, which disintegrated when my hand disturbed the dishwater.
— *C. L. Bore*
Redwood Falls, Minnesota

O'ercast was the moon, and howling like a banshee the wind on the night when, on a richly panoplied bed in her castle tower, under the bifurcated wings of the House of Hapsburg, the Countess Lillo deSpanola, Princess of Turin and Taxis, gave birth to her only child, a daughter, who, despite the nobility of her station, was destined to become world renowned in softball (slow pitch).

—*Donald Edge*
Cherry Hill, New Jersey

LYTTONY V

CALL ME ⸺

"In the year 18— I settled as a physician at one of the wealthiest of our great English towns, which I will designate by the initial L⸺."

—opening sentence of
A Strange Story (1861)

⸻

Morning's innocent light disclosed fresh blood staining the still-sleeping children's mouths as Monica, in horror, removed their leaf-strewn pajamas and the anklets of brass bells from their tiny feet, knowing that, again, they had been abroad in the night following the strange old nun from house to house in their pleasant upper-income suburb singing eldritch songs of plant worship and performing grisly rituals of blood-drinking and Morris dancing.

—*Gretchen S. Ellis*
Houston, Texas

Staring glumly at the corpse, so carelessly, so insultingly, so nakedly tossed on the trash pile behind the administration building, President Henrietta—Mother Hen to her students—wondered painfully what this contretemps would do to her plans for funding advanced training in computer programming.

—*Richard E. Haswell*
Springfield, Missouri

Understandably, he rode like the wind, and this was because he was in a hurry, but the horse grew refractory and jettisoned him,

like a jack-in-the-box on a drunken binge, into the lobelia by the
roadside, where the fair maiden found him with a sprained ankle
execrating the creature that hurled him there, and crying a pox
upon it and the world in general, most specifically Guy de Brais-
bun, from whose cuckolded wrath his ungentlemanly retainer
was fast fleeing, in the dubious hope and expectation of keeping
his manhood intact.　　　　　　　　　　　　—*Robert W. Shields*
　　　　　　　　　　　　　　　　　　　　　Dayton, Washington

"My name be 'Ortense LaFitte, an' I be French-Canadian by
birt', work in de mills in Quebec all my life, an' I wish now to tell
of de biggest t'ing dat ever 'appen in Quebec, or so my modder
she say, when I was leetle girl, too yong to remember."
　　　　　　　　　　　　　　　　　　—*J. Thompson*
　　　　　　　　　　　　　　Rochester, New Hampshire

Handsome, strongly muscled, but lean as a rapier, splendid in
his colorful bolero jacket, silver-trimmed leather pants, and enormous sombrero, his cruel mouth curled in a sardonic smile, his
hooded dark eyes flashing as he gazed at the faces of the motley
crew he called his *compañeros,* he reined in his horse so that the
magnificent beast stood toweringly on his hind legs—truly a su-
perb picture of the legendary Mexican *bandito,* El Loco.
　　　　　　　　　　　　　　　　　—*Louise M. Laval*
　　　　　　　　　　　　　　Albuquerque, New Mexico

On the second of September, 1948, fiftieth anniversary of the
Battle of Omdurman, Davina Sturge-Browne was safely brought
to bed of a fine boy (as her great-grandmother the first Countess
of Poole, a leading beauty of her day, would have put it) after
twenty-three hours' labour—"the only labour we tolerate around

here," quipped her brigadier husband, who was Joint Master of the Netheravon Foxhounds, as he left at daybreak for the first cubbing of the season, secure in the knowledge that in twenty years this youngster, too, would be an Old Wimbornian,

> Holding Wimborne's honour high
> 'Mid storm or battle's flame,
> For statesmen fall and nations die
> But Wimborne's aye the same.
> —*Patrick Haldane-Stevenson*
> *Canberra, Australia*

Was this gorgeous vision with the jaunty nurse's cap and the proud breasts really the pesky tomboy he remembered from back home before the war? wondered "Ack Ack" Ackerman as he deliriously fingered his Distinguished Flying Cross in a bed at the evacuation hospital in Bongo Bongo.   —*Black Jack Ramsey*
Madison, Wisconsin

When you nursed me in the lap of your luxurious smile, I sprang savagely to life, ready for war, with my purple, ah! blue patriotic blood thunderously soaring, spiraling through melting flesh.   —*Joseph Anderson*
Staunton, Virginia

Alexandroyurivitch Nevtsoshostakhievnich yawned drowsily in the early morning light and looked content-edly at his enormous wife, Elieyenadobranevska, sleeping soundly beside him, when suddenly he noticed a longish blonde hair stuck ominously to her puffy upper lip, mov-ing up and down rhythmically with each wheezing breath she took.
—*Mary A. Harrison*
Marietta, Georgia

After adjusting his old-fashioned spectacles over his aquiline nose Pyotr Petrovich Ulyanov perused the cryp-tic note from his Moscow advocate Ivan Nocolaevitch Kaminsky, hinting of the long-predicted troubles at his heavily mortgaged estates in the Vkase district, and real-ized simultaneously that K in Petrograd must be chortling over the myriad implications and S in Odessa (the bounder) had doubtlessly consummated his implied threat to inform Barishnykoff's mistress about the complicated and unseemly affair between the notorious Masha and the *arriviste* Captain Nijinsky (né Goldberg) which would sig-nify reverberations from Pinsk to the Turkish frontier, and pique the curiosity of certain advanced circles in Paris long accustomed to harping on the so-called agrarian problem.
—*Bernard J. Packer*
San Pedro Sula, Honduras

It was a bright and cheery day; the rays of the amber-hued sun (for in the cloudless sky this rounded orb emitted arched frag-ments of prismatic glistening ambience) marched soldierlike

through the vast battalions of the eastern heavens, sounding, as it were, a clarion call to each and every one who heard the echoes rippling through dawn's throaty abyss, to wake once more the somnolent world from its drowsy sleep and, with muted trumpet voices, proclaim the entrance of the new-hatched day, proceeding as does chick from egg, and standing in precise military formation to salute this hot and fiery star, the herald of a just-published page in the calendar of their lives, lives made more grandly bearable by the sure knowledge of Old Sol's daily rearing of its sparkling head in the eastern reaches of the upper atmosphere—in short, dear reader—for my palsied hand grows weary with much writing—the sun did rise!   —*Shirley Cook Wuolle*
                                          Sarasota, Florida

"MANDY,
THE DUCK!
THE DUCK!"

OR AT LEAST IT FALLS
WITHIN THE PARAMETERS
OF A FAIR COUNTRY APPROXIMATION

" SCENE, *The Hall in Uncle Roland's Tower*
TIME, *Night*—SEASON, *Winter*.
Mr. Caxton is seated before a great geographical globe, which he is turning round leisurely, and 'for his own recreation,' as, according to Sir Thomas Browne, a philosopher should turn round the orb, of which that globe professes to be the representation and effigies."
—opening sentence of
My Novel (1853)

Old man Lewis sat bolt upright in his bed at precisely 3:16 a.m. on the night of the Academy Awards ceremony, when most of the celebrities were back in their own or each other's posh homes, sampling exotic pharmaceutical concoctions, and screamed, "Mandy, the duck! The duck!" as his heart shuddered to a long-overdue halt.
—*James McGuire*
Worthington, Massachusetts

As the half-dozen ballet students whirled and twirled around the hall, turning in penché turns around and around, Corwin realized suddenly with really no warning that Hilletat, the dance student next to her, was turning at more than one-and-a-half times the speed Corwin was doing, and at that rate, Hilletat would probably crash into Corwin in just a few more seconds.

—Antoinette Dwinga
Carnegie, Pennsylvania

Roger Duncan balled his fist into a large muscle, saying to himself, "Darn! I coulda raised rabbits instead of these stupid geese!"

—Lorilee Howard
San Francisco, California

Lena Glynn stretched her short little legs that dangled 5 inches above the floor because the chair in which she was sitting was not made for undersized little people, who are not quite dwarfs, but yet not considered average height.

—Frances Moss Moore
Dayton, Ohio

The race may belong to the swift and the applause to the rapier wit, but what accolades are heaped upon the heads of the well-intentioned?

—Carol Ann Webb
Atlanta, Georgia

Heather Pennymore gave away her sun dress, as well as her last dollar, to a half-naked, yet pious-looking, crone who was babbling to herself in the public square, and even as she did this

Heather thought to herself, "Holy cow! did I pick up this huge bruise on my thigh during the wrestling match, or did I thump it against the doorjamb while beating my hasty retreat from the boys' locker room, and do I have a last tuna at home in the lazy Susan for supper tonight, since I am now quite penniless?"

—*Michael D. Houlihan*
Stevens Point, Wisconsin

"Charles," she pronounced Frenchly, elevating him far above all the other Chucks on Forty-second Street who were not sipping Grand Marnier in the balmy summer breezes.

—*Frances H. Shaw*
Saint Petersburg, Florida

It was a wonderful day, a chirpy day, the kind of day that makes even the sickly homeless derelicts sing zippity-doo-da as the girls go by in their scanty skirts and a little boy watches his brand-new Japanese kite break from its string and sail into the cloudless sky, vanishing from sight, traveling freely without restraints, towards an unknown destination which the boy's father (a self-ordained priest now living in Mexico with a retired madam named Maggie) usually called "Eternity."

—*Howard Camner*
Miami, Florida

As had happened other evenings in the past—not every evening, to be sure, but this evening in particular—as I reclined in my easy chair to contemplate the events of the day (some good, some bad; all in all a fairly unremarkable day and quite comparable to many others) over my before-dinner brandy, which I had come to prefer over my favorite of previous years—scotch and soda, mixed on the strong side with only a little ice—it occurred to me that perhaps I should again propose to Alicia despite the fact that on at least one previous such occasion that I could recall she appeared to have fallen asleep before I had quite finished.

—*E. Ward Nommensen*
Houston, Texas

The tall, nervous young man in his car in Oklahoma was considering cutting his toenails while his middle-aged, overweight mother in her apartment in Massachusetts was thinking of cutting her hair, when by some petty, insignificant, meaningless coincidence, both mother and son suddenly thought of husband and father (respectively), who was contemplating cutting his wrists in his bathtub in California.

—*Mary K. Bradford*
Daly City, California

"Fingernails—they grow so fast—I'm always having to do them!" cried Ursula, as she sat filing hers by the light of the waning afternoon sun.

—*E. D. Bryan, M.D.*
Dover, Delaware

There was a sadness about him, sort of as though his mother had told him when he was very young that he was poor material for life and he had taken it to heart.

—*Vicki Walsh*
Petersburg, Alaska

Though they are not as glamorous as the intrepid officers of the Highway Patrol, the people who collect taxes, albeit not the stuff of which heroes are made, nonetheless have their own exciting adventures to recount, so allow me, if you will, to lead you through the routine day, week, month, and year in the life of a tax auditor of the California State Board of Equalization.

—*Sid Mandel*
Carmichael, California

A black chip of desiccated vinyl ablated from the top of Rich Mooney's '65 Impala and drifted in the Mojave Desert wind to rest on the shoulder of Highway 15 next to a flat Coors can somewhere between his vertiginous bald tires and last night's Las Vegas motel. —*Mario J. Vasquez*
Long Beach, California

Her eyes filling with crystalline drops, she turned to Cecil and gasped, "Indeed, sir, I never gave you cause to anticipate my affections in any but the most sisterly manner and yet," her white eyelids fluttered, scattering tiny diamond tears onto his silken cravat, "your insistence on the return of a greater warmth is not entirely unwelcome." —*Sue Williston Khavari*
Bayside, Wisconsin

"But my dear," he began, decanting the amontillado to within a blessed inch of the crystal rim rising in splendid concavity above her faintly flushed fingertips, "have you carefully considered that the decline in the use of the subjunctive, which you so beautifully prefer to the garden variety indicative, has indeed contributed to the decline in manners which you have, just now, so forcefully asseverated—hmm?" —*Richard H. Rupp*
Boone, North Carolina

"Aw, hell!" groaned the contessa who, up to that point, had shown no interest in the conversation.   —*T. Manning Powers*
Rome, Italy

"Life is full of decisions," laments the corpulent jeweler Sam Flambard, still wet from the hot tub, chamoising himself briskly while reflecting on life's major idiosyncrasies to his blind (poor thing) pet parrot, Wanda, whose only response is a bland elongated c-h-i-r-p.
   —*Ron Peer*
Phoenix, Arizona

Randall, with his very most indignant expression, quaveringly replied, "That parrot means absolutely nothing to me!"   —*Donna L. Hurth*
San Jose, California

The scimitar of the sun was separating shadow from reality as Hilbert's stallion thrashed through the desert sands bringing him ever closer to understanding and disclosure of the hitherto obscured vision which had seemed impenetrable, yes, even imperturbable.   —*Benjamin S. Roberts*
West Palm Beach, Florida

TODDY TWORF
THE
MORPETH
DWARF

AND A GENTLEMAN OF
NO SMALL FLATULENCE

"Sir Peter Chillingly, of Exmundham, Baronet, F.R.S. and F.A.S., was the representative of an ancient family, and a landed proprietor of some importance."
—opening sentence of
Kenelm Chillingly (1873)

<hr>

Since I'm the all-knowing Private "I" (Eye—ha, ha!) in this novel mystery, I'm telling you, the reader, who the killer is right now so you can enjoy knowing who he is *as you read along:* it's Toddy Tworf (the Morpeth Dwarf). —*Lucy Lightbody*
Troy, Michigan

The most interesting feature about the Reverend Erin F. X. Nagobods, besides the swollen, bulbous nose planted pinkly between ruddy cheeks, above a tightly drawn mouth, and below dark, deep-set eyes, was his name. —*Gregory J. Budzien*
Wauwatosa, Wisconsin

Perdita Nerrdbigger grimly waited in the Greyhound station, Rupert's biting sarcasm of that morning filling her mind and steeling her resolve to scrape out a career for herself in the city as a dental hygienist; she swore that she would claw, tooth and nail if necessary, to the top of her profession, and then she would return one day and guffaw in his face. —*Gineva M. Malliet*
Fort Meade, Maryland

Polycarp Jones was the biggest football player anyone at Rumney State had ever seen; when he ran (and oh, how he could run) the ground trembled; when he fell (which was often and cataclysmic) the coach trembled; it was like watching Goliath being felled by his own untied shoelaces—because in addition to being the biggest and runningest football player in the world, Polycarp Jones was also the clumsiest.   —*J. Thompson*
Rochester, New Hampshire

Both of the other clerks in the file department chewed over it for days afterward: how Bernadette Filz, normally so reliable about putting the insurance claim cards promptly in alphabetical order, nevertheless grinned just a touch recklessly at the end of this one Friday lunch hour, moistened her fingertip with that shocking pink tongue of hers to crumb the last pumpernickel bits off her desk blotter, and then impishly dialed Weather, for no other reason on earth than to assure herself of an uneventful ride home on the bus for a weekend jam-packed with TV watching.
—*Virginia Wolf*
Kroge, West Germany

Call me Ishmael, or call me Hezekiah, or call me Jethro, or call me Obadiah, or call me Nahum, or call me Nebuchadnezzar, or call me Habakkuk, or call me Zephaniah, or better yet—don't call me, I'll call you.   —*Linda Hutton*
Coeur d'Alene, Idaho

"What I really wanted to say," said my uncle Ignatius Ponsonby Dreck, smoothing his time-ravaged locks, "while courting the not inconsiderable hazard of repeating myself—you may have heard me on the subject once or twice before, assessing the respective merits and demerits (for instance) of railway stocks last

Monday, or was it Sunday?—and, although I would naturally be extremely mortified if you dubbed me a bore (regarding it as grossly unfair!), nevertheless, it can bear repetition, I feel, at least once more; a man's talents, his intrinsic worth, can no more be accurately measured by his bank balance than by his receding hair."
—Douglas Livingstone
Durban, South Africa

Rodney Clive Barnstable-Kamehameha was trying again, as he had been most of his adult life, trying, trying, trying; among those he numbered among his few friends, it was generally agreed (and those he numbered among his few friends generally agreed on very little) that Rodney (or Sugar, as he was known to those numbered few) was the most trying person any of them knew, and they often wondered why they were themselves numbered among his few friends. *—James A. Perkins,*
Richard L. Sprow
New Wilmington, Pennsylvania

HAIRY
PROTEINS AND
ARTIFICIAL
SWEETENER

WELL, MAYBE ONE OF THE
WINDOWS WAS HALF CLOSED

"It was towards the evening of a day in early April that two ladies were seated by the open windows of a cottage in Devonshire."   —opening sentence of
Alice; or, the Mysteries (1838)

~~~~~~

Yes, Cathy could ingest a full-grown rat when she was in the mood, then wash down the rodent with great quantities of diet cola (when she knew perfectly well one shouldn't mix hairy proteins and artificial sweetener).   —*Rix Quinn*
Fort Worth, Texas

"Say cheese," the graying and stooped man muttered through buckteeth while his pinkish pointed ears and elongate wirelike whiskers twitched with excitement over the irony of that command made to a group which had come to his studio to be photographed, and which, after all, had no reason to suspect that he was descended from rats.   —*James H. Roberts III*
Arlington, Virginia

He clutched her slender, heaving, naked body to his chest and stood, sweating and filthy, upon the sands while the charging ravenous eaterbeast neared and he screamed out a challenge, "Come and get it while it's hot!"   —*Kitty Drew*
Salinas, California

The ritual slaughter of the anteaters traditionally took place on the longest day of the year. —*D. E. Cunningham*
Placentia, California

Gently they rocked their chairs in contrapuntal cadence to the cacophonous chirping of crickets and croaking of frogs, those denizens of the Atascadero Home for the Aged, as they dislodged from their dentures the residual shreds of the rutabaga casserole they had eaten for dinner, and, with a sigh, one lamented aloud, "Oh, for those halcyon days when we were continent!" as a shot rang out, felling the poor soul.
—*Sid Mandel*
Carmichael, California

He was a Portuguese who had never fished and she was a Chinese who couldn't cook rice; he had enough hair on his chest to make a coat for a very small Hungarian and the way she kissed it made him wonder why. —*Don Austin*
Vancouver, British Columbia, Canada

The web of suspicion tightened around the gaunt, haggard figure of newcomer Schuyler Scrugman, as Eulice Screep, the petite Welcome Lady widow of Owl's Hollow, swore she saw ten fingers stacked like miniature cigars in Mr. Scrugman's smoky lavender tobacco jar, as if fresh and neatly chopped off at the knuckles at Olaf Weigstrand's market in the village.
—*Ray Clark Dickson*
Cambria, California

"Fancy meeting you here, Miklos," said the gentle-looking old gentleman seated on the wooden park bench, slightly raising his eyes without interrupting his self-imposed task, repeated every afternoon at the same hour, of feeding bread crumbs and bits of eggshells to the usual crowd of rustling, milling pigeons: "Eggshells are pure calcium; they are very healthy because they aid digestion, and in addition they help the birds lay robust, hardshelled eggs, which is no mean accomplishment."

—*José A. Lourenço*
Lisbon, Portugal

"Ugh!" said Dir, an average Australopithecus robustus, as the saber-toothed tiger raked Dir's stomach with a massive paw only an instant before instantly dying as Dir's club smashed the big beast's skull into something resembling scrambled egg, colored red.   —*David Meltzer*
Mabelreign, Harare, Zimbabwe

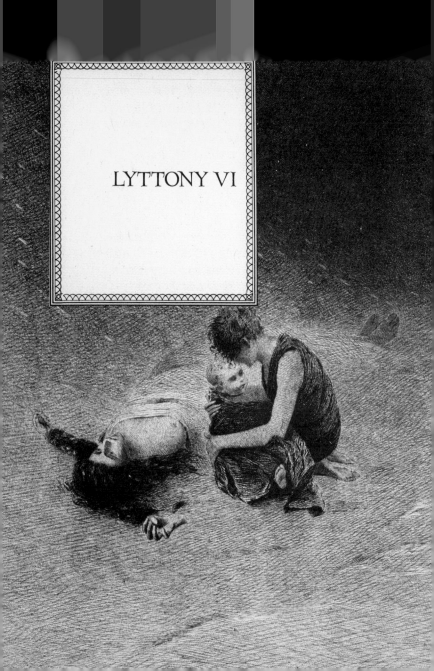

LYTTONY VI

EITHER THAT, OR
IT WAS IN ONE OF THE
UGLIEST IN DEVONSHIRE

"It was a summer fair in one of the prettiest villages in Surrey."   —opening sentence of
What Will He Do with It? (1858)

The Litany of the Sidars of Labanon flowed through my (murky) stream of consciousness beyond that (demolished) blue and white hotel on the snowy peak of paradise, as Eva, my nine-year-old nubile daughter, afraid neither of skiing, flying, or dying, swallowed Adam's apple in a Freudian slip of her tiny, titillating tongue, and then pelted me with blood-red rosebuds wrapped to look like balls, of butter, of course.

—*Harold M. Blumberg*
Zichron Yaakov, Israel

The dark countenance of the swarthy, mustachioed villain was split by the white flash of a lecherous grin as he looked gloatingly on his fair captive, whose unavailing struggles with barbarous bonds had left her in an alluring state of dress-disorder—"Ah! Ah!" sniggered he in French, as he spoke fluently the language of the corrupt courtier, "what price your vertu now?"

—*Henry Bourgeot*
Lycée Français de La Marsa, Tunisia

From the fragile farming land around Dimboola, in northeastern Victoria, the rapacious, searing wind gathered the parched topsoil and bore it, whirling and gusting over the arid farms and burning forestland, to the very throbbing heart of the state's governmental and financial capital, Melbourne, where it blotted out the streetlights and flung power lines together, causing blackouts in thousands of homes and galvanizing the inhabitants' brains into recalling the immortal words of Ava Gardner: "Melbourne is the right place to stage the end of the world."
—*Lois Conrick*
Toowoomba, Queensland, Australia

Digger waved the cloud of bush flies away from his narrowed blue eyes, eyes wrinkled at the corners from many hours of staring at sun-browned horizons, pushed back his old slouch hat with its strings of corks to the back of his sun-bleached hair with a tanned hand, muscular from many hours of humping his bluey, and drawled in a nasal twang to his companion black tracker: "Stone the crows, Didgeri, me old cobber, time we drove that old man kangaroo off into the mulga."
—*Margaret Curlewis*
Coburg, Victoria, Australia

Lydia was the youngest in a family of nine children, and each of them was to play an important part in her growing-up years—all the way from Ronald, the eldest, who was her first lover, and

Barbara, who was her second lover, all the way down to Becky, the "Middle Moffat" as it were, fat and shy and vicious, who eventually discovered and exposed Lydia's relationship with Ronald and Barbara, all the way down to Dwight, closest to her in age, whom she finally ran away with to a commune in Idaho; this, then, is Lydia's story.   —*J. Thompson*
Rochester, New Hampshire

Butch Andrews sat in a waterfront dive and belted down another shot of rotgut—his eleventh of the night, or maybe it was the twelfth—he couldn't remember, he couldn't remember anything but Maria—Maria, the wide-eyed, virginal French girl who had nursed him back to health in the basement of the bombed-out convent after he had been wounded fighting for the French Resistance, which he had left his home in Ohio to join, but it was all a dream to him now.   —*Sondra Rouse*
Farmington, New Mexico

Sinuously, she sneaked her way on little cat's paws until she spied her loathsome lover with his snarling mastiff, the leering devil who had brutally deposited the unborn child within her, the grinning gargoyle who had fiendishly infected her with the dreaded Herpes II virus; and raising her pearl-handled pistol, she fired, faster than a speeding bullet, into the depths of his sprawling back porch.   —*Janice Gay*
Concord, California

Safeway wasn't open when Keegan pulled his Chevy into the lot, its valves chattering, gun-blue cracked-ring smoke sputtering from its tail pipe, to get eggs.   —*George V. Griffith*
Chadron, Nebraska

"Call me, Ishmael," chirped the hoary bimbo as the hulking sailor stumbled out of the ramshackle flophouse, "before you leave Rangoon!" —*Mary A. Harrison*
Marietta, Georgia

"Though your girl friend is a friend of mine, call me, Ishmael, any time." (from *Sailor's Delight,* the bawdy memoir of a prostitute working in a Nantucket brothel during the height of the whaling period)
—*Tony Staszek Mattis*
Sunland, California

THE
BOULEVARDS
OF
LAREDO

I SEE BY YOUR OUTFIT THAT
YOU ARE A COXCOMB!

" 'Ho, Diomed, well met! Do you sup with Glaucus to-night?' said a young man of small stature, who wore his tunic in those loose and effeminate folds which proved him to be a gentleman and a coxcomb."

—opening sentence of
The Last Days of Pompeii (1834)

━━━━━━━━━━━━━━━━━━━━━━━━━━
XXXXXXXXXXXXXXXXXXXXXXXXXXXXX

"Bang, bang, bang, bang, bang, bang, bang," smiled Black Bart as he emptied his six-shooter into the drunken Injun whose blood gushed out like little red oil wells. (from *The Boulevards of Laredo*)
—*Wayne Wenning*
Celina, Ohio

Jim stepped out of the bunkhouse, his boots in his hands, looked up at the morning sun already hot enough to fry eggs on a saddle horn, shook a scorpion out of each boot, spat tobacco juice and watched it sizzle on the ground, scratched his belly, and said, "Looks like it's going to be a nice day."
—*Edwin Z. Crawford*
Sacramento, California

A red rubber balloon of a western sun, pricked by a finger of saguaro cactus, sank behind the purple mesa as Mosey Long spurred his snorting, sweating, spavined, slab-sided sorrel toward the sinister shadows spreading across the sands and whatever un-

welcome that lay beyond. (from *Nine-to-Five Cowboy against
Ten-to-One Odds*)   —*Henry Henn*
                                                 Pacifica, California

A cowboy should know his horse, but it seemed to the podners
at the Triple Q Ranch that Vernon McChew had gotten *too*
close.   —*Beloved Remington*
                                         Newport Beach, California

Rex Spurr sat so tall in his saddle that the Mexicans didn't
know if he was a god or a saguaro cactus, and who could say that
they cared, given the torturous temperature which the fireball
sun beat down on the frying-pan-flat landscape, like pellets of fire
raining from the mouth of a volcano, but this was not Hawaii, no,
this was Texas!   —*Jim Heiden*
                                          Stratford, Connecticut

As the dusty rider crested the ridge, he paused his horse and
let him blow, meanwhile pulling the brim of his salt-stained and
droopy Stetson low over his eyes, the better to scan the valley
below, but quickly taking his silhouette off the rim by jerking the
reins back and left as the whine of the ricochet spanged his gut,
the shock coming from the scrabble near his mount's off-hoof—
too close, he felt, to the cracked remnants of the time-ravaged
scruff of his favorite right—and only other—boot.
                                         —*Donald Duane*
                                          Buena Park, California

The grizzled old camp cook, painfully aware of the roping ac-
cident thirty years ago which had cost him his job as trail boss and
the love of Sheila, the beautiful, half-breed dance-hall girl, limped
to the fire and spat into the frying pan, testing its readiness for

biscuit baking, oblivious to the polysyllabic lowing of the nervous, fitful trail herd, which sensed the impending arrival of a dark and stormy night.   —*H. Winton Ellingsworth*
Tulsa, Oklahoma

Seen through the stinking smoke of a smoldering straw-strewn saloon, the setting sun looked like a sorrel sack of soggy stogies, as stocky Stanford Stubbins, the Stanislaus Stampeder, stiffly staggered from the stuffy stagecoach; stonily stood in startled stupefaction; spontaneously saluted the still-standing Stars and Stripes; sternly stepped over the struggling scorpion; silently slew the slithering sidewinder; sadly swallowed the single swig of sickly-sweet sarsaparilla; sullenly shrugged his shrapnel-seared shoulders; suddenly stopped staring at the stolen stirrup; and sorrowfully saddled the sole surviving starving stallion . . .   —*Jay J. Levine*
San Francisco, California
Winner, Western category

HEAVING
ALABASTER
BOSOMS

OR IS IT
"BUXOM WERE THE LASSES"?

"Merry was the month of May in the year of our Lord 1052. Few were the boys, and few the lasses, who overslept themselves on the first of that buxom month."
—opening sentences of
Harold, the Last of the Saxon Kings (1848)

His dark eyes embraced her heaving alabaster bosom as the moonlight enshrouded them completely and the pulsating fury of the ocean battering Carmel's already beaten coastline heightened his sense of desire.
—*Roxanne Savage*
Carmichael, California

The moon glowed above, a milky orb whose shape and luminescence echoed that of Veronica's bosom showing through the bodice of the dress torn in her struggle to escape the count (there was a time when she would not have struggled, but that was before she knew his dark secret), as she paused briefly, gasping for breath, listening for the footsteps of her pursuer—that symbol of oppression: the great white male.   —*Sue Katz*
Auburn, New Hampshire

"La, Sir Reginald!" cried Lady Sylvia, "I should be *vastly* obliged if you would remove your hand from my bodice!" and with those words, coyly delivered with an arch smile, she rapped the naughty baronet's venturesome hand with her fan.

—*Angelica Peale*
Radnor, Pennsylvania

"I'll never marry again," she vowed, clutching her small fist to her perfect, pear-shaped breast, narrowing her feral green eyes, watching her remaining friends bear the overelaborate, heavy coffin of her latest husband, Mervin, down the long, sparkling white gravel drive to the manicured, green cemetery of the Griftwood Estate, knowing soon they would see her beauties, the heirs of her immense fortune, all two billion dollars of it, the only ones who really cared, who really loved her, her three hundred, carefully tendered, pampered cats, and then she slowly closed the door, never to open it for the next eighty years.

—*Terry Gallavan*
Santa Ana, California

She felt his intelligent hands roaming across her slender supine body, pausing to trace the front of her blouse where the tiny pearl buttons formed a *V* around her shapely breasts, the fingers moving like his own fine horses to her waist, where they traced the jagged track mark that his carriage wheel had made when it caught her from behind as she fled towards the forest with her valise, and the last three years rose in a misty turbulent cloud before her dimming eyes when she heard his playful far-off voice scolding, "And your best silk blouse, too, my dearest one."

—*Carol Collins*
Santa Ana, California

"Just because you saved my life doesn't mean you have a claim on my body," the brilliant cosmetics tycoon Vanessa Van Camp

coldly informed her calculating neurosurgeon, Rex Mailer, as she decisively pulled her tailored jacket over the filmy blouse, which revealed the sensuous outlines of her voluptuous body—but did her smoldering dark eyes flash the fire of a different, more primal message?
                                                              —*Nancy Linder*
                                                              Madison, Wisconsin

The searing white heat of the desert was stirring Purity to consciousness; she opened her swollen emerald eyes, her semi-nakedness amid the disheveled ruins of her velvet gown, her thick Titian tresses matted with the perspiration of terror and her tears of passion a startling sight to the group of peasant women gathered round her after she had been deflowered by the cruelly handsome bandit that she so vehemently hated, but also secretly loved.
                                                              —*Dee Flour Knott*
                                                              Glory Hole, Colorado

Lisa Truck, lately distraught, her proud and opulent bosom thrusting with renewal, knew that Ann—dearest, Dear Ann—would advise, would sympathize, and so with firm resolve she took the pen and padded to the sofa, to couch those stomped-on feelings she shared with "Kangarooed in Kankakee."
                                                              —*McBinge McMurphy*
                                                              Las Vegas, Nevada

Her heaving bosom rose and fell like twin boiling suet puddings at Epsomtide, gleaming in the low glow of the incredulous candelabrum, bursting the straining fabric of her wildly embroidered kimono.
                                                              —*Barbara Carthorse*
                                                              Seal Beach, California

It was a Gothic scene extreme: the richest mahogany, the proudest flowers, the sideboard with flickering, nay, glittering, nay, seductively shimmering candles enhancing the brave décolleté of Lady Grande (for she was of the type generally described as generously endowed), and as she raised her gloved hand to greet Sir Mann, he gasped . . . for, forsooth, of a surety, said brave décolleté, suddenly succumbing to perhaps what could have been the wardrobe master's worst, or best, nightmare, gaped.

          —*Mary Adams Phillips*
          Panama City, Florida

Puzzled by the hidden bounty behind her red frock dress, the small elfin creature picked up the scissors lying by the bedstead and began to cut gingerly in concentric circles, careful not to plunge the device into her more delicate flesh, but he was nervous.

          —*Richard Hardack*
          Bronx, New York

"Baroque am I, beleaguered, and bereft," moaned Elenore, the ecru rosaline point on her ocher velveteen gown a companion to the rococo swirls of cherubs, acanthuses, and gilded volutes bordering the oval mirror which reflected her powdered, corkscrew-curled hair with its lovelock, vermilion spots resting on her high cheekbones, a hint of chinoiserie on her ivory fan; as suspirations heaved her bosom and hints of lachrymosal dew dampened her dark orbs, and she contemplated the dastardly, portly scrivener Phineas Pinchpenny, who waited without to discuss her financial state and to suggest a means (private, he leered) through which she could settle the tangled finances left by the early demise of her husband, the late Lord Randolph-Huntley-Richmond-Moneypacker III.

          —*Betty Kikumi Meltzer*
          Beaumont, California

With an almost imperceptible, but still perceptible, though she may have thought it imperceptible, flick of her tiny, blue-veined, but alabaster-white wrist, Monica Forthwright tugged discreetly at the left strap of her lemon-yellow, string bikini top, causing her ample endowments to swell, tremble, quiver for a tiny, an almost imperceptible, but still perceptible moment, and then settle softly back into their frail vessels like two bowls of not-quite-yet-set warm tapioca set suddenly down side by side on a cold kitchen counter, and glanced with dark and stormy eyes over the top of her opalescent and polarized and very, *very* expensive sunglasses at Brad, who was *still* not there. —*Daniel J. Brown*
San Jose, California

VILE PUNS

THE ONLY MAIL THEY DELIVER TO ———— IS MARKED "OCCUPANT"

"I am a native of ————, in the United States of America."   —opening sentence of
                        The Coming Race (1871)

XXXXXXXXXXXXXXXXXXXXXXXXXXXXXXXXXXXXXX

Pamela's heart beat fast and her hands trembled a lot as she listened to the intermittent knocking on the front door of her shanty located near the railroad tracks beside a hobo jungle, and she thought, "That's a bum rap if I ever heard one."
                        —*Frankye D. Thompson*
                        Astoria, Oregon

The railroad agent told the Navajo, "The coming of the Iron Horse will bring great prosperity to the Redman," but the Indians had reservations.   —*Jon Williams*
                        Guthrie, Oklahoma

He was a dark and swarthy Templar, an errant mongrel who asked, when shown the large, ugly canine of questionable lineage designated his steed to carry him into the dark and storm, "Surely, knave, you would not send a knight out on a dog like this?"   —*Herbert H. Hulse, Jr.*
                        Houston, Texas

As the ancient Japanese warlord samurized the situation, he could lop off the man's head but that act of pique would only make the man smaller in his eyes.   —*Stephen M. Dobbs*
San Francisco, California

The long, sensitive fingers of the world-renowned concert pianist slid sensuously over a different instrument—the gracefully curved and finely tuned young body of his current traveling companion and source of artistic inspiration, a dabbler in the arts by the name of Celeste Schwartzkopf, who sighed luxuriatingly, "Reggie, darling, that was *divine*—but *do* try that Chopin Nocturne in E-flat minor again—only a little *lower* this time!"
—*Nancy Linder*
Madison, Wisconsin

"Take your hand off my breast!" she tittered.
—*W. R. C. Shedenhelm*
Encino, California

In the room where Bulwer-Lytton sat, stroking his toad, the cock never crowed, nor the clock never ticked but clucked, "Dickens, Dickens, Dickens."   —*Stan Fullerton*
Santa Cruz, California

She stood there, wanly and nakedly, a rose shorn of her petals, and then he plucked her again.   —*Sam Kaplan*
Ann Arbor, Michigan

"The leg, he is fractured," he said in broken English.
—*J. Baumbardner*
San Jose, California

Amy the Safecracker—Being the novel short story of the amiable Airedale that is truer than fiction who dogged the guard into the kitchen, nosed open the safe, and, picking out the pie and butter, padded out the door, and when returning the guard saw her tail and picked up the scraps of aluminum pie tin from the floor and knew he'd been foiled again.   —*D. L. Harris*
Houston, Texas

It was a stark and smarmy night as I gathered my thoughts to call in to the editor the events of the twister that knocked down power lines, and I had a deadline to meet, and I met it there at the knocked-over phone booth.   —*Harriet K. Doyle*
Hyattsville, Maryland

She stood there in stockinged feet, her shoes set askew with wagging tongues and laceless eyes—their worn and leathery faces giving silent reproach for the abysmal state into which she had plunged their soles.   —*Elaine McAnnany*
Edina, Minnesota

The Great Barrier Reef is 900 miles long and Wilmer Chanti, the great explorer, says it could be circumcised in forty days.
—*Edward L. Hurle*
Rye, Victoria, Australia

When I turned the key to open my lab door, I thought it would be my usual dull day, until I noticed that my little *cucaracha* (genus *Blatta*) had flipped over on his back, frantically waving his little legs, and I realized that someone had bugged my bug.   —*Winona Van Etten*
Ellensburg, Washington

Nathaniel, having judged last night's séance as only medium, realized the need for greater rationality in his investments and decided to try some of the booming nuclear power industry stocks. —*Anthony Rosler*
Elsternwick, Victoria, Australia

They were at the Harley Queen Ball and soon it would be nigh unto midnight, the witching hour, and Kristin would behold the unmasked face of this ravished creature—she of the form divan, who made all of his muscles genuflect, his heart palpate, his head ruminate; oh, he had waited so very long for her, in fact, all of his seventeen years, and now, now, he felt hoary with desire.
—*Renée O'Brien*
Seattle, Washington

It was a sark and dormy night, its green clarity diluted by my roommate who, as usual, was making cutting remarks as she drank my scotch. —*Sandy Lawrence*
Kalamazoo, Michigan

It was the best of wursts; it was the worst of wursts. (from *A Tale of Two Bagels*, a novel about a Jewish delicatessen owner during the French Revolution) —*Nils Peterson*
Campbell, California

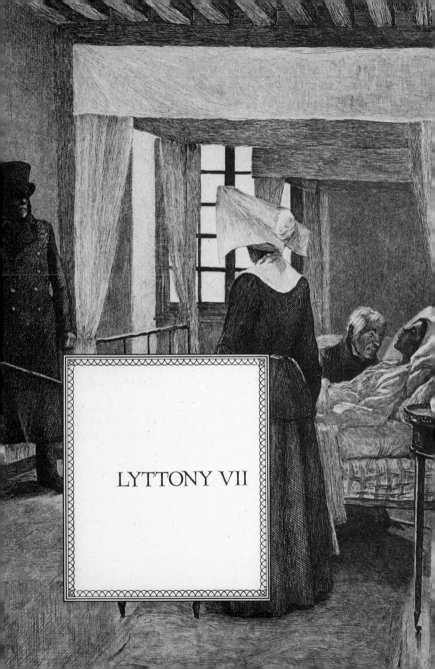

LYTTONY VII

AND WAXED AND MULTIPLIED . . .

"At Naples, in the latter half of the last century, a worthy artist named Gaetano Pisani lived and flourished."
—opening sentence of
Zanoni (1842)

<hr>

"Good morning!" exclaimed brisk, hearty George Bruce as he strode into the dining room on a bright, sunshiny morning in early spring following a cold winter, and then again, "Good morning to all!"
—*Mary Webster*
Oak Park, Illinois

The bright sun peeked gaily through the early morning's scattered clouds, its rays glistening merrily upon the refreshing, pure, morning dew on the golden waving wheat, as smiling, plump Mrs. Brown called her hungry brood from their appetite-whetting chores to a breakfast of peppery scrambled eggs, lean crisp bacon, syrupy buckwheat flapjacks, cold foamy milk, rich hot coffee, and buttery light biscuits, marking this as yet another richly rewarding day of noble, productive labor on the family farm.
—*Rev. William F. Charles*
Saint Louis, Missouri

It was a nice day and cheerful Nellie busily dried the breakfast dishes in the nice kitchen.
—*Nancy J. Brousseau*
Philmont, New York

A sudden, violent shower washed against the hog barn and, as quickly as it began, it stopped, and now the warm sun dried the land in the valley of the Medicine River, bathing miles of young wheat with nourishment; I stepped back, pausing to fill my senses with the splendor and excitement of another Nebraska summer day.
—Donald L. Barnhart
Jekyll Island, Georgia

Whining and cringing had been good friends to Willie Fisk.
—Harvey G. Young
Decatur, Georgia

With unusually cloudy acumen Jerome came to his realization: first, that life offered few breath-sucking moments, and, second, that this wasn't one of them—today portending in fact to be another of those rummy passages in time in which he would again be asked to bite not only the bullet but the drool- and wheat-germ-laden teething ring of his nubile, mal-cloned niece.
—Richard Swanson
Madison, Wisconsin

There was no way Elron could have foreseen that Sheila would bear him five sons, as he watched the childlike woman skip about the steward's cabin chattering nonsense—five sons who all were to marry hand-me-down women and bring up children they never fathered.
—Estella Kohler Leppert
Tallahassee, Florida

"It's another Jonestown," Sam Springer's steel-trap computer of a mind deduced as he scanned the hideous grins on the bodies of the disarrayed and very dead judges of the Second (and obviously last) Annual Bulwer-Lytton Contest; but first, he knew,

he would have to decipher the cryptic and uncompleted message written in chalk on the blackboard: "There but for the grace of . . ."   —*John Paul Vancini*
                                    Brooklyn Center, Minnesota

To truly understand scuzzy ol' Mortimer Fatback, that cruelly deformed gnome, Valium addict, convicted procurer of handicapped high school coeds, and crippler of slow-moving puppies, one had both to begin and to survive the frequently foul and invariably tedious task of tracing back over his ninety-four-year existence; from the dilapidated collection of Quonset huts in the hills of northern Trenton, where his mother abandoned him while still in labor, all the way through to the hash parlors and hamburger joints of Port-au-Rancid, Vermont, site of the darkened street corner and wildly careening transit bus that cashed in his chips for him on that blustery, long-ago December evening.
                                    —*Don Stacom*
                                    Rowayton, Connecticut

"Call me a schlemiel," grinned the toothless Benny Rozman at his motley crew of derelicts as his shrimp boat headed out under the Golden Gate for the choppy waters of Bodega Bay 32 knots south, "but today we're gonna forget about fishing and find us the wreck of the *Princess Magellan* . . . and the gold and heroin that went down with her."   —*John Paul Vancini*
                                    Brooklyn Center, Minnesota

On that fateful morning, the incandescent sun burst brightly above the solemn mountains, illuminating the awe-inspiring dark forest that John Dear found himself racing through, the vial clasped loosely but safely in his frozen hands, with but one thought in his head as he stumbled again and again over the irri-

tatingly rough landscape, and that thought was as old as time itself, the need, when all other needs are but shadows of their former selves, the need to destroy, and by destroying, rebuild, and,
therefore, John did not have the presence of mind to see the root
looming out to trip him, sending the vial of precious fluid shooting out of his hand, smashing against a rock, and changing all of
humanity.   —*Gary Firestone*
                                  Regina, Saskatchewan, Canada

   The dust had settled into the lined and weary face of Rex
Winthrop as baby powder settles in between the toes, as he
slowly straightened his aching back in the dusty half-light of the
Egyptian sunset, staring, enraptured, at the mummified remains
of the Egyptian princess; at her protruding cheekbones with the
dried skin flaking away; at her brown and ragged teeth showing
through the shapeless mouth; at the craters of eye sockets gazing
into an era of ancient ritual; and Rex finally faced the haunting
fear that had hovered over his heart from his youth: This was the
woman he could have loved, only—he had been born too late.
                                  —*Laurie Smith*
                                  Yardley, Pennsylvania

   She'd never make it, Ida thought, as she shielded her face with
her arm and turned her head sideways glancing momentarily toward Helga, who fondled her red underpanties whilst she considered whether she should jump off the Havre de Grace
bridge—perhaps tomorrow—where it arched over the B & O
tracks or over the Susquehanna River, but at that very instant,
Tomjohn Pritchitt, attempting to land his hang glider on the
grass of Hyman Park, collided with the electric company's low-
hanging wires and burned both hands off at the wrists, and while
he dropped toward the ground screaming, the pain and scorching

odor brought back his first memory of fire—hallucinating with half a tab of Mr. Natural acid still lodged under her tongue, his mother had dropped half a joint of Colombian Purple Hair into his crib, which landed between his legs, blistering his uncircumcised penis—and as he crumpled on the ground, the bus smashed into Ida, the driver having glanced away, after ogling Helga's bare legs and the red satin underpanties she manipulated between her thumb and first finger, to watch Tomjohn crash and burn.

—Keir Van Tassel
El Paso, Texas

What can you say about a twenty-five-year-old manatee that died?

—William MacKendree
Paris, France

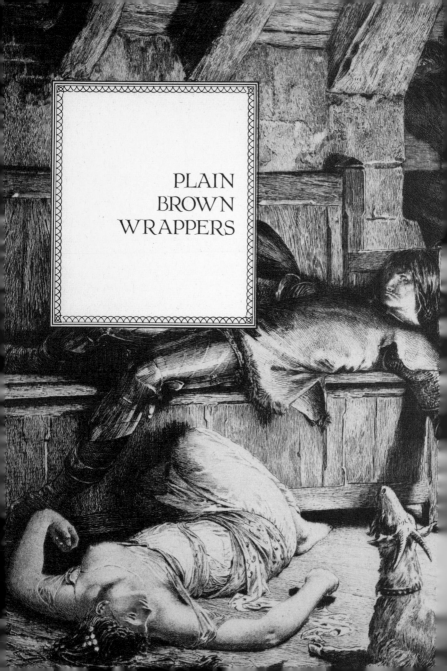

PLAIN
BROWN
WRAPPERS

BECAUSE **** LIVES THERE
WHOM I LOVE TO ****

"In the county of **** there is a sequestered hamlet which I have often sought occasion to pass, and which I have never left without a certain reluctance and regret."
—opening sentence of
Eugene Aram (1832)

It ain't easy to be a teenage girl, let me make that clear to you right off the bat, as it was to me, Ginger Del Veccio, the first time I laid my baby-greens on the bulge in Stan Steele, Herkimer High's new high school geometry teacher's, pants and thought, "Bring on those 45-degree angles!"   —*Cynthia Miller*
Minneapolis, Minnesota

She was in tropical heat.   —*Richard Lowe*
Wilmington, Delaware

Of the circumstances under which she had written an unpublished thesis comparing the Lower Paleolithic hand axes in the Lynch Hill Terrace of the Berkshire Bank of the Middle Thames with those in the equivalent terrace on the Buckinghamshire Bank, she decided to tell him nothing—not, that is, until she had got him into bed. (from *Man and His Tool: The Anguish of a Feminist Prehistoric Archaeologist*)   —*Shelley Cranshaw*
Oxford, England

Kathy had it all: power, wealth, and fame; but as she looked down at the adoring, upturned faces of her board of directors, she knew she could never have what she wanted most—an orgasm.

—*J. Jason Matthews*
Madrid, Spain

Maeta removed the cigarette obstructing his mouth with its obscene, fluorescent glow, and flicked it into the tray with a gesture of victorious exaltation that would have outdone Caesar glorying in a triumph, as she dropped her face on his and smashed her tongue into it till it met his in an erotic shock that sent his hands exploring the full length of her naked body, causing him to stiffen so dramatically that his organ thrust through his open fly, defiantly shaking its reptilian head in a flagrant outburst that threatened her virtue and virginity with irretrievable destruction, although she slyly snickered to herself because she had nothing that sanctimonious to lose, and was, on the contrary, nourishing both her vanity and her vagina by initiating the chauvinist foreplay, punctuating it with an "oh, oh, OHH!" that caused the cat in the basket beside them to litter prematurely in the midst of her vibrant leonine murmurs.

—*Robert W. Shields*
Dayton, Washington

Her eyes burned into him with the force of a jackhammer and he quickly disintegrated into the pavement of her flesh.

—*Herself A. Eu*
Redondo Beach, California

Malcolm knew what everyone thought of him, but the days of being the four-eyed bookworm were gone and he was charged

like an eel biting a fuse box as he carefully loaded the supposi-
tories with the sensitive, heat-activated nitroglycerin.

—*Steve Garman*
Pensacola, Florida

Sadly ... actually, no, it was with more of a derisive melancholy that he turned away from *her* as he methodically but not
unclumsily buttoned up his trousers, buttoned them, you see,
since he was not only old-fashioned in his dress (zippered Jor-
dache jeans forbid!) but as much so in his mores, which was why,
if truth be told, he was feeling more than a modicum overcome
by a slathering guilt over his bestial activities, now finished, with
the *woman* who lay there on the bed in the dank closeness of the
room clutching a dirty sheet to her pendulous breasts as she
reached for a filter-tipped cigarette, lit it, inhaled deeply as she
tossed her sweat-soaked hair over her right shoulder and glar-
ingly mouthed the words, "Get the hell out of here, you wimpy
bastard, since above all else, you are the type to make one fairly
ill!"

—*Thomas H. Schulz*
Beverly Hills, California

The message in her eyes was unmistakable and the heaving of
her bosom gave away the secret of her inner turmoil, causing him
to catch his breath and take a stumbling step foward, at which
movement she whisked a snub-nosed revolver from her bodice
and snarled between clenched teeth, "Take one more step, you
sonuvabitch, and I'll blow your balls off!"

—*L. Mathews*
Bloomington, Minnesota

On their wedding night 230-pound but svelte Gloria, her
gnarled toe caught in her greasy pantyhose, fell gushing onto the

water bed while Buford, lovesick with Ripple, felt his prostate swell in anticipation of the delights to come.

—Dennis E. Minor
Ruston, Louisiana

She felt claustrophobic, crushed by the moist essence of strangers' bodies: musky, fragrant, rancid, clean, dirty, like the odor of freshly turned humus and the dank smell of dark, wet places.

—Jamie Henderson
Fairfax, Virginia

Casting an eye over his shoulder, he threw her bodily upon the bed, ripping off her clothes with one hand and fumbling with his jammed zipper with the other, their panting breaths coming as one impassioned sibilance, their ardor dampened only by her spike heel puncturing the water bed and their bodies cascading around the room immersed under 200 gallons of water.

—Leo Simon
North Hollywood, California

Scratch, scratch, scratch; scratch, scratch, scratch—that's all I heard in a year of sleeping with a veterinarian.

—Nature Johnston
Jacksonville, Florida

I was dry and he was hard, which about sums up the marriage, in more ways than one.

—Cynthia Miller
Minneapolis, Minnesota

At last—it was their long-awaited wedding night, for which, in celebration, Lily demurely opened up her forty-year-old port, while James eagerly indulged in cider.

—R. Eugene O'Kiks
Vallejo, California

Her breasts hung like spent liverwurst casings and moonlight played upon her thighs like two tennis players engaged in a mortal combat to the death. —*Robert H. Fugate, Jr.*
Chicago, Illinois

The bright morning sun effortlessly penetrated the gauzy-curtained window and caressingly fingered the rumpled form still wrapped in contented sleep as Howie, glancing back with remembered satisfaction, slipped his belt through its buckle, mechanically lifted the stiff lever, and deftly maneuvered it into the second opening. —*S. L. Freed*
Silver Spring, Maryland

A
DARK AND
STORMY
NIGHT

AND THE RAIN FELL IN
MY WHISKEY GLASS,
DAMPENING MY SPIRITS

"It was a dark and stormy night; the rain fell in torrents—except at occasional intervals, when it was checked by a violent gust of wind which swept up the streets (for it is in London that our scene lies), rattling along the housetops, and fiercely agitating the scanty flame of the lamps that struggled against the darkness."

—opening sentence of
Paul Clifford (1830)

It was a dark and stormy knight who stood rigidly at the cliff's edge, scowling out over the cruel sea, and ruggedly bracing himself against the fierce winds which howled in from the west, where a ship had appeared suddenly on the horizon, silhouetted sharply in the long, snaking claws of lightning that crackled in over the cliff to freeze Sir Richard's saturnine, chiseled patrician features in sharp relief, etching the look of shock that registered his alarm at the sound of the shot that suddenly rang out, above the furious cacophony of the storm.

—*Peter Shann Ford*
Miles, Queensland, Australia

It was a dark and stormy night in old London-town but halfway around the world in romantic faraway Calcutta, dawn was just peeking in the window as the intrepid alpinist Montmorency Blankinsop (Mont Blanc to his many friends) rose wearily from his troubled bed, still undaunted and determined that this day he would climb the bewitching but ever-resisting Fanny Hill.

—James P. Collinge
Rochester, New York

It was a stark and dormy night; the coed streakers ran from hall to hall (for it is on a state university campus that our scene lies), except at occasional intervals when they were checked by security officers who were rattled and fiercely agitated by the inflaming sight of the rain-streaked, flashing white, yellow, and black bodies, the last-named seen only in the scant, intermittent alabaster illumination by the now-and-then bursts of lightning.

—Anthony Harrington
Marietta, Georgia

It was a dark and stormy night; the sailors were gathered 'round the camp fire and the captain, rising, his earring vying with the diamond insert in his gold front tooth for the firelight's reflection, and grinning salaciously at the captive Lady Imogene, said, "Come, lads, we'll have a story from this little piece here—and a rollicking one, too—or we'll disembowel her children before her eyes and then, laughing ourselves hoarse while she screams, we'll betake the edge of gloom off this God-rotting night!"

—James R. Kickham
Garden Grove, California

It was a spark and dormy night in the firehouse bunk room and the taking of a burned-out fireman's poll had left them, all extinguished men in their field, up in the air, suspendered, and panting for the alarming results.

—Herbert H. Hulse, Jr.
Houston, Texas

It was a hot and brilliant day; the sun burned down mercilessly—except at occasional intervals, when it was blocked by a vagrant cloud which had been pushed into position by the tepid breath of wind which lazily strolled up the streets (for it is in Rochester that our scene lies), rolling along the asphalt and docilely licking against the lolling tongues of the dogs that struggled against the heat. —*Robin N. Leatherman*
Rochester, New York

A full 50 leagues from Reading, on the bleak Welsh marches, the Lady Morwynneth, slumbering in her lofty bedchamber hard beneath the encorbeling of the northwest tower, soon to become known to all posterity as Maitland's Folly, was startled from fitful oblivion into an uneasy yet curiously eager wakefulness by an unearthly moaning and bestial slavering, which at first had seemed as she awoke to have been uttered by no more than the gibbering gnomes populating a nightmare occasioned by a tardy surfeit of mead and winkles, but which she now knew could only be issuing from the crazed lips of some living creature poised a few short paces from her couch and hidden from her sight by the silken curtain brought by camel and ass from far Cathay to guard her against the chill night air and prying eyes, and reached out with only half-fearful fingers to draw back the curtain, gasped, not at the nocturnal chill, but with a thrill of joyful dread, as she beheld, silvered by the moonlight streaming through the exiguous slit of the chamber's solitary loophole, not merely the prying eyes, but the complete incarnation of her most frequent and pressing prayer, for at long, long last, it was a stark and horny knight! —*Graham Padgett*
Saint Norbert, Manitoba, Canada

It was a dark and stormy night; black storm clouds raced before the moon like ghost riders across the sky, the wind wailed like a banshee, and the leaves whirled around me like dervishes, as, sick with fear, and almost sightless in the ghastly light, I watched in horror my own true love caught in the clutches of the shuddering, trembling, bottomless bog.

—*Mary S. Suydam*
Kings Beach, California

It was a dark and stormy night; the rain plastered the cheap dress enticingly to the backs of my legs, as I bent to scrape the still-warm gum from the sidewalk.   —*Jeanne M. Shultz*
San Francisco, California

It was a dark, stormy night and the rain blew in blinding blivets across the Rue de Boulevard, where I ducked into the wet, rotten plaster-smelling doorway of a decaying baroque building; and thought to myself, I have been a lot of places, seen a lot of things, and had a lot of reasons not to believe in God, but Maria Elena was not one of them.   —*Richard Coram*
Fairhope, Alabama

The marquis was a dark and stormy knight, and as his flashing eyes burned into Jessica's and he crushed her against his broad chest, her bodice with the delicate lace flowers in lilac shades all in disarray, raining hard kisses on her warm, yielding mouth, her auburn tresses shone in the glow from the fireplace in the gloomy mansion, and the rising, pulsating tides that pounded in her heart made her swoon into his iron arms, and a small moan escaped from her crimson lips, "No, no . . ."   —*Fred Manget*
Atlanta, Georgia

She loosed her dark and stormy hair, which tumbled down her naked back in a torrent of rage-tossed waves billowing in a violent cascade, except for patches of silvery shafts here and there (for it is on a moonlit night that this event takes root), at last spending its fury in a few stray wisps, and fell to her gleaming buttocks. (from *Mistress of Brutel-Wylton*)

—*G. B. Johnson*
Walnut Creek, California

It was a dark and stormy night and rain fell on every house in Piscataway—Piscataway is not large and the torments of weather most often affected all its residents at like times, unless someone happened to be visiting his aunt in Hackensack, where the weather is worse; both cities being frequently agitated by power failures due to storms, which leads one to the realization, undampened by the sogginess from water in the clothes, shoes, and even the brain of this writer, that being in the dark in London is much the same as being in the dark in Hackensack, not to mention Piscataway.

—*Dennis McDougle*
Miami, Florida

It was a dark and stormy night; screams echoed loudly throughout my mouse-manure-encrusted family manor as my beautiful and fragile child bride, Dahalia, struggled mightily with the racking agony of a difficult first labor, until I finally could stand it not one minute longer—so I stormed to the door of her room, flung it open, and exclaimed, "Heave on her, doc, it might be twins!"

—*Sandy Bitner Brown*
Guymon, Oklahoma

ENTER THE BULWER-LYTTON FICTION CONTEST

The Bulwer-Lytton Fiction Contest is an annual event that asks entrants to compose the worst possible opening sentence to a novel. Anyone anywhere may enter. The rules are simple:

1) Sentences may be of any length and entrants may submit more than one, but all entries must be original and previously unpublished.
2) Entries will be judged by categories, from "general" to detective, western, science fiction, romance, and so on. There will be overall winners as well as category winners.
3) Entries should be submitted on index cards, the sentence on one side and the entrant's name, address, and phone number on the other.
4) The deadline is April 15 (chosen because Americans associate it with another painful submission).

Send your entries to: Bulwer-Lytton Fiction Contest
Department of English
San Jose State University
San Jose, CA 95192-0090